Land of Shame and Glory

PETER HENNESSY

Land of Shame and Glory

Britain 2021–2022

First published in 2023 by
Haus Publishing Ltd
4 Cinnamon Row
London SW11 3TW

Copyright © Peter Hennessy, 2023

A CIP catalogue for this book is available from the British Library

The moral right of the author has been asserted

ISBN 978-1-913368-88-3
eISBN 978-1-913368-89-0

Typeset in Garamond by MacGuru Ltd
Printed in the UK by Clays Ltd, Elcograf S.p.A.

www.hauspublishing.com
@HausPublishing

The Publishers are grateful to *The Economist* for their kind permission
to reproduce the excerpts on pages 23, 78, and 85.

For Cec and Poll,
daughters and joybringers

Contents

There were days in winter when the sun barely seemed to rise above the rooftops before running out of juice. On those days, the light stayed on in his flat from when he woke up until he retired for the night – same went for the heating. They were saying on the news that bills were about to shoot up. Rebus reckoned he would be okay, but others wouldn't. Politicians would say the usual things while wringing their hands. Whole bloody country seemed to be fraying and its inhabitants along with it.

Ian Rankin, *A Heart Full of Headstones*

Acknowledgements

Producing a diary-based book is a novelty for me. It's been a slightly unnerving mixture of the pleasurable and the painful.

The pleasure comes from a pair of sources: the satisfaction of the daily discipline of writing it with its intellectual stretching required to try and catch the debris of the day while making sense of it, and the context of its aeronautics as it flies by. The pain arises from the sheer awfulness of recording the brutalities of war abroad while, at home, the country one loves underperforms as a society and polity with example after example of wretched behaviour on the part of one particular prime minister unsuited for the highest office.

It was also an adventure enlivened by good companions. My wife, Enid, and my daughters, Cecily and Polly, on whose judgement I perpetually rely (although it doesn't always look like that to them). My publishers and friends Barbara Schwepcke and Harry Hall at Haus – our collaborations always punctuated by much laughter; my former student, Matt Lyus, whose eyes are the first to fall upon my prose as he converts my handwriting into text and now does for me what I used to do for him – marks my work. I am also grateful for the meticulous care of my editors Ella Carr and Jo Stimfield.

My friends at the House of Lords Library are, as ever, a great comfort to someone whose little grey cells and gifts (if that isn't too presumptuous a word) as a hunter-gather of information are not quite what they once were.

Finally, only since ill-health has required me to spend more time at home, have I come to realise how much I depend everyday on BBC Radio 4's so-called 'sequences'. As for the quicksilver, the incomparable Paddy O'Connell, brings to 'Broadcasting House' on Sunday mornings, I thank him not just for his friendship but for provoking me to let fly with fusillades in words that, but for him, would have been kept locked away in my little library in Walthamstow.

Standards High and Low

As we look for new answers in the modern age, I for one prefer
the tried and tested recipes, like speaking well of each other and
respecting different points of view; coming together to seek out the
common ground; and never losing sight of the bigger picture. To me,
these approaches are timeless and I commend them to everyone.

Queen Elizabeth II, centenary address to the Sandringham
Women's Institute (WI), 24 January 2019[1]

I am the last bastion of standards.

Queen Elizabeth II, 1992[2]

Monarchs, unlike prime ministers, do not write manifestos – any
more than they pen their own epitaphs. Certainly, it would hardly
have been Queen Elizabeth's style. Had she been tempted to craft
a disguised one, however, it might have sounded like those telling
words she spoke to her fellow members of the WI.

For in those few sentences, over tea and cakes with friends on a
winter's afternoon in north Norfolk, she described the values that,
together, had been the lodestar of her life. At the same time, she
held them up as a guide not just for her successor but for all those
engaged in the national conversation, indeed to society in general.
'I commend them to everyone,' she said simply. For her, it was a
template on how a country should be run and a people respected. I
thought those words were quite powerful at the time she delivered
them. They remained so – very much so – when we pondered the

coming kingdom in the days after her death, which scored a deep line across the page of British history. For, with her passing, 2022 became the last year of the post-war era.

It was also a year of extremes in standards: the lady carrying the very loftiest was laid to rest in her family vault in St George's Chapel, Windsor, on 19 September; the man exhibiting the lowest was finally forced out of 10 Downing Street on 6 September. It was, for the British people, a year 'crowded with incident',[3] as Oscar Wilde's Lady Bracknell might have put it, beyond the fall of a prime minister and the demise of a sovereign.

The economy shuddered. The supply chains carrying the food to sustain our bodies and the fuels to warm them stretched and frayed. We worried. We recriminated. We fell out with each other. Finally, we came together in grief and loss when Queen Elizabeth II died at her beloved Balmoral Castle on Thursday 8 September 2022 at the age of ninety-six. She had been her kingdom's fixture for seventy years, while around her so many of the country's fittings had changed. As the Queen herself expressed it after the atrocity of 9/11, 'Grief is the price we pay for love.'[4]

On the afternoon of Friday 9 September, the new monarch, King Charles III, welcomed the new prime minister, Liz Truss, to her first audience in Buckingham Palace, telling her that losing his mother was 'a moment I've been dreading, as I know a lot of people have'.[5] Many of us had. We had talked quietly among ourselves about it more and more since the Covid pandemic first struck her kingdom in March 2020. *Please do not leave us; this is not the moment to go. See us through.* She did see us through three more times: through the pandemic; through the unseemly endgame of a constitutionally rogue premiership.

The third time she came through for us was after her own death. Her absence reminded us just what kind of country we can be at our best through the values she carried with her every day of her reign – duty and service, burnished by a brand of humility and a brand of understatement all her own. As King Charles III talked to country and Commonwealth in his first address, at his Accession Council, and in his words to both Houses in Westminster Hall, the third bequest became quite apparent – those sterling qualities are both timeless and transmissible. They were Queen Elizabeth's last great gift to an anxious nation itching to think better of itself and more optimistically about its prospects. This was something that I sensed powerfully in the days between her last breath in Balmoral and her final laying to rest in Windsor.

For years to come historians will seek to extract the flavours of 2021–2. Herein lies a modest, early attempt. It was the writer E. L. Doctorow who said: 'The historian will tell you what happened. The novelist will tell you what it felt like.'[6] This book is shaped by a diary – one person's highly imperfect attempt to mix the two, which, in a sense, is what diaries are for. Of its nature, it's a precarious task. I hope it's worked.

Peter Hennessy
Walthamstow, South Ronaldsay, and Sheffield, 2023

INTRODUCTION

Taking the Pulse

Recent history races towards us at high speed; earlier history
accompanies us at a slower, stealthier pace ... early history – long-
distance history – ... invites us to reflect on history with a slower
pulse-rate ... when it comes to the present day, with all its different
potential dénouements, deciding which are the really major
problems essentially means imagining the last line of the play.

Fernand Braudel, *A History of Civilizations*, 1995[1]

The joy of the historian's craft is that there never is a 'last line of
the play'. The 'major problems' are hardly ever solved. Ameliorated,
yes. But rarely fixed. The joy of the chronicler is twofold: the task
of historical capture and storage is deeply fascinating; its infinite
ingredients mean that we shall never be out of work unless or until
the human race loses its curiosity about how we came to be as we
are and where we might be going – 'that thin wisp of tomorrow
which can be guessed at and very nearly grasped', to quote another
Braudelism.[2]

Every year, in the late summer, I tend to succumb to an appetite
for a wider-perspective history, while in Orkney in our 'granny flat'
overlooking the ever-temperamental waters of Scapa Flow, where
the light, the wind, and the weather change with an incontinence
that only the clash of a sea (the North) and an ocean (the Atlantic) can generate. The summer of August to September 2021 was no
exception.

There were two 'problems' that technically bore the label of 'long-distance history' – their origins both date-stamped in the eighteenth century – that were nonetheless pressing their faces against our huge picture window in South Ronaldsay with the urgency of recent history. One was climate change (it was around 1750 that our islands initiated the world's first Industrial Revolution fuelled by coal, powered by steam, and marked by copious quantities of hugely damaging carbon emissions). The second was the Scottish question – the political future of the landscape and water in front of me (the result of the Act of Union in 1707).

A third problem circulating during the summer of 2021, Covid-19, was still relatively new but threatening to become endemic, and regrettably part of a 'long present' rather more than a 'thin wisp of tomorrow'.

And finally crowding in to claim their place at this time were the other national problems that I wrote about in this book's predecessor volume, *A Duty of Care*:[3] social care, social housing, technical education, the preparation of our economy and society for the growing force of artificial intelligence, as well as the difficult and demanding pathway to recovery from our first Covid experience.

At the end of July 2021, there was already a great deal to recover from. On 26 July, one week on from the so-called Freedom Day, when nearly all Covid-related legal restrictions in England were lifted, this was the statistical picture:

Total deaths: 129,158
Long Covid cases: c.1 million
1 in 100 of the UK's 66 million population has Covid
Estimated lifetime cost of government's Covid measures:
    £372 billion[4]

At the end of the first week of 'freedom' the government's Social Mobility Commission reported:

Across the UK there are already signs that attainment gaps

between advantaged and disadvantaged children are getting wider. Every critical measure of low social mobility – child poverty, income inequality, access to stable housing, unemployment for young people and gaps in school attainment – was poor in 2019. The impact of Covid-19 is threatening to make each of these factors worse.[5]

I noted in my diary entry for Monday 19 July: '"Freedom Day" is better described as "Anxiety Day"'. A YouGov poll in *The Times* suggested that public opinion shared this view – 55 per cent thought ending restrictions was wrong; 31 per cent thought the Johnson government was doing the right thing.[6] In his book *Spike: The Virus vs the People*, published in the first week of 'freedom', Sir Jeremy Farrar – director of the Wellcome Trust – pointed out that on a global scale:

> There is no natural law governing when the next outbreak will arrive, who it will affect and how catastrophic it will be. A virus could leap across from animals to humans somewhere in the world and begin spreading tomorrow, or later this year, or in 2024. Our urbanised, interconnected world is custom-built for pandemics.[7]

This was the brutal lesson we had all (or nearly all) learnt since March 2020. If anything, in late July 2021 we felt a greater sense of danger-past and peril to come than of recovery taking hold – even when the figure for new cases unexpectedly fell for six consecutive days between 19 and 25 July.[8]

July 2021 also marked the second anniversary of Johnson becoming prime minister and his fitness for office – the 'Boris question' – was as acute as ever. On the night before he went to the palace to see the Queen and accept her commission to form a government, I said to the broadcaster Michael Cockerell in a profile he was preparing for BBC2's *Newsnight*:

There is a spectrum of opinion about Boris Johnson. One is that he will be the most unsafe pair of hands ever to open a prime ministerial red box. And at the other end people think here is a man of brilliance and flair. I veer to the anxiety end of the spectrum – because you cannot busk being prime minister.[9]

Two years later, when Michael was completing his book *Unmasking Our Leaders: Confessions of a Political Documentary-Maker*, he asked me if I had changed my mind. I said I hadn't, adding, in the context of Johnson's style of government and his lack of sensitivity towards constitutional conventions:

You cannot expect Mr Toads to obey the highway codes. The particular skills he brought to the job of winning elections were of no use in facing a pandemic. But he did have a fresh chance when he came back from intensive care, knowing at first hand just how awful the virus was. It could have been his shining hour – to move from being a party leader to a national leader. But he hasn't done so. The problem is that it's a totally performative premiership: it's all about him creating the building blocks for his own legacy.[10]

The greatest exponent of the art of the political cartoon of our time – Peter Brookes of *The Times* – captured the Johnson problem far better than I ever could in prose in his 'Short Supply' on 23 July 2021, on the back of the story of supermarket shelves emptying as retail staff were being 'pinged' by the Covid app in increasing numbers.[11]

The wider question raised by the Johnson premiership was whether he was the manifestation of a political equivalent of climate change – a coarsening of political conversation, a growing disregard for the conventions and decencies of government and the constitution. Or was he an aberrant one-off? Either way, the Mr Toad of UK politics was absolutely tone-deaf when it came to the necessary self-restraints or states of mind needed to operate the British state (the 'good chap' theory of government).[12] In terms of the wider national political conversation, it was plain that the '"infodemic" of misleading assertions' would continue unabated[13] alongside what the writer Jenny McCartney calls the 'outrage inflation', which is 'a key element in the Twitter economy'.[14]

On the real, physical question of climate change, the first week of 'freedom' also saw the publication of a report by the Royal Meteorological Society warning of a wetter, hotter kingdom to come with frequent 40-degree heatwave summers and more freak weather events in a way that caught the imagination of the headline writers ('"Average" weather in Britain is a thing of the past, say experts').[15] Our islands are going to be baked, battered, and rinsed to a degree we have not experienced before – one of the few things we can be certain about.

The society's report on the 'State of the UK Climate 2022' drew on long runs of data to trace our road to serious climate instability:

LAND: 2020 was the third warmest year for the UK in a series from 1884. All the top 10 warmest years in that series have occurred since 2002. The most recent decade (2011–2020) has been on average 0.5°C warmer than the 1981–2010 average and 1.1°C warmer than 1961–1990.

PRECIPITATION: 2020 was the UK's fifth wettest year in a series from 1862 with 116% of the 1981–2010 average and 122% of the 1961–1990 average rainfall.

SEA-LEVEL RISE: Mean sea-level around the UK has risen by approximately 1.5 mm a year on average from the start of the twentieth century, excluding the effect of vertical land movement, resulting in an overall rise of 16.5 cm over that period ... The rate of sea level rise has increased recently, exceeding 3 mm [a] year for the period 1993–2019.[16]

These findings were vividly put into global perspective when on 9 August the UN's Intergovernmental Panel on Climate Change published its 'Code Red' report on the 'unequivocal' link between human activity throughout the industrial era and the vast bulk of global warming – of which more shortly.[17]

To adapt the libretto of Haydn's *Creation*, the heavens were telling the story to come on land, sea, and in the air, because the weather, at least, was one aspect of national instability we could measure as it had happened – or was happening – and make reasonable predictions as to its future in the coming decades as a direct consequence of carbon emissions past. The severity of these predictions will depend on whether or not the global community reaches the targets agreed in Paris in December 2015 and in Glasgow in November 2021.

The fate of the post-1707 Anglo–Scottish Union, however, is quite another matter. Ever since the 2014 referendum resulted in Scotland staying in the Union (there was only 10 per cent in it), I had carried a sense of peril within me that by the mid-2020s we could see it gone, a fear greatly sharpened by the Brexit referendum result in 2016 with Scotland voting 62 per cent to remain and England 53.4 per cent to leave the European Union.

Boris Johnson's constitutional tone-deafness extended to 'The Land of the Mountain and the Flood' when he said, in a context where he must have known it would leak, that devolution to Scotland in the late 1990s had been 'a disaster north of the Border' and 'Tony Blair's biggest mistake'.[18] His appointing himself 'minister for the union' was perhaps the greatest irony of his premiership.

There was, however, one member of his Cabinet who *did* have a real sensitivity towards Scotland – Michael Gove, chancellor of the Duchy of Lancaster in the Cabinet Office and the minister with responsibility for devolution and constitutional affairs. There was a touch of a modern-day John Buchan about Gove, the son of a family in the fish trade in Kittybrewster. His was the classic rise of the scholarship boy via Oxford to a high position in the state, 'the nearest thing we have to a lord of the Isles at the Cabinet table', as I described him when he came to give evidence to the House of Lords Constitutional Committee (of which I was then a member) on 20 July 2021 (the day after 'freedom' was declared).

Michael Gove was, I think, the most intellectually interesting member of Johnson's Cabinet – and a much better phrasemaker than his boss. He deployed some polished evocations before us:

> The union is not an historical artifact. It is not a dry set of con-stitutional arrangements. It is a living, breathing success story ...

> The most important thing about the union is to recognise that it is a family of nations and a nation of families, and if we concentrate solely on the constitutional wiring then we miss the bigger picture ...

> This is a story we cannot leave to others to tell. We have to ensure that we are continually updating it and making it sing.[19]

One of the interesting things about Mr Gove's evidence was that he accepted it was his job to make the Anglo–Scottish Union 'sing' and that if the committee 'are not hearing it, that is my fault'. There-upon, he promptly sang to the committee quite a song about his conviction that:

> there is something about the historically loose and baggy nature of Britishness that is of great value, because in a world where the diversity of a nation's population is a source of its strength, being able to be proudly British and proudly Scottish, proudly gay and Welsh, proudly Jewish and Northern Irish, all these things are an example of the direction that states want to go to make the most of the opportunity available to their people.[20]

He acknowledged, too, that an understanding of Scotland had deteriorated in the years of 'devolve and forget' after I had cited evidence the committee had received from Philip Rycroft (former constitution director in the Cabinet Office)[21] and Michael Kenny (professor of public policy at Cambridge) that we had become something of a 'kingdom of strangers'.[22] 'Your point', said Gove, 'is a fair one overall in that I think there has been a retreat in the mindset ... in understanding every part of the United Kingdom equally. Respect for the devolution settlement – genuine respect – has become a case, exactly as you say, of devolve and forget.'[23]

In a reply to Baroness Drake on the 'case for constitutional reforms', Gove betrayed a typically British aversion to treating constitutional affairs in a systematic manner – to seeing it as a unified whole, as opposed to an accumulation of historical accretions:

> I am a Tory. I have to confess it. 'Out of the crooked timber of humanity, no straight thing was ever made.'[24] Tories recognise that in constitutions there will be knots in the wood. Tory constitutions are not IKEA. They are made from oak and ash and pine and fir.

Michael Gove couched his remarks in a Tory tradition. But he spoke, I thought, for the deepest of shared conventional wisdoms in Cabinet and Whitehall committee rooms ('an historical overhang ... no bad thing' was how he expressed it) when he declared before the Lords committee, 'These constitutions reflect our past – and human nature. They are resilient, and that is why a desire for perfect constitutional perfection and symmetry is, I think, not really very British.'[25]

Gove's elegy in a (virtual) Westminster Committee Room was a tour de force. And for all that he suffused it with Toryism, it was recognisable to anyone who has observed or thought about the mysteries of what Simon Case, the Cabinet secretary (and a former PhD student of mine) had earlier described before the committee as our 'weird and wonderful constitution'.[26] Yet one of the big questions about the 2020s, as the second Covid summer glided into autumn, was whether the UK would experience an event – or a sequence of events – that might challenge Gove's vision of an adaptive, resilient constitution that flows on without design or plan. It would take a great deal for us to shift from being what Philip Ziegler called 'a sort of back-of-the-envelope type' of people.[27]

On Sherlock Holmes' famous sliding scale of difficulty, designing a systematic British constitution is a three-pipe problem – something no government has yet attempted. It may be that our historic aversion to capturing it and formalising it in a grand compendium of a single document is, for us, a British equivalent of Holmes' Giant Rat of Sumatra – 'a story for which the world is not yet prepared'.[28]

In the summer of 2021, the British prime minister wasn't prepared either – not for any kind of constitutional reform, let alone a big one. On 5 August during a visit to Scotland (his first for seven months) he said: 'Constitutional change is about as far from the top of my agenda as it is possible to be.'[29] He delivered this perhaps counterproductive remark – given where it was made – a few days after Michael Gove said that a second independence referendum would happen if it were the 'settled will' of the people of Scotland.[30] (Alister Jack, secretary of state for Scotland, later refined 'settled will', explaining that polling data would need to show over a 'reasonably long period' that 60 per cent wished a second referendum to take place.)[31]

Scotland abandoning the Union would, in my judgement, require the remainder of the UK to, as it were, reach for all three pipes and a large box of Swan Vestas and get on with it. The danger would lie in the exhausting complications and dreary, will-sapping processes that separation would involve, leaving us even more averse to constitutional thought and innovation – a torpor almost amounting to a blight on a shorn kingdom.

By the summer of 2021, I had come to the reluctant conclusion that we could not simply sustain our old romantic view of the efficacy of the British constitution, in all its uncodified majesty, nor the belief that out of its peculiar and always unplanned growth something of a self-adjusting beauty and suppleness had emerged.

One aspect of national life that seemed to be going well in the summer of 2021 was sport: the European Football Championship was closely followed by the Tokyo Olympics, both delayed from 2020. As a bonus, the England football manager, Gareth Southgate, drafted a 'Dear England' letter to calm the tense arguments about identity and his team 'taking the knee' after the murder of George Floyd in the United States.

He told his players to remember 'you have the opportunity to produce moments that people will remember forever. You are part of an experience that lasts in the collective consciousness of our country.' In the letter he sings a patriotic tune, extolling the values that his grandad – a proud Second World War veteran – instilled in him, of having pride in one's country ('The idea of representing "Queen and country" has always been important to me'). 'But, despite all the changes in modern football,' he continued, 'what cannot be questioned about the current generation of England players is their *pride* in representing this country.'

As for those who racially abuse some England players: 'Why would you choose to insult somebody for something as ridiculous as the colour of their skin? ... You're on the losing side. It's clear to me that we are heading for a much more tolerant and understanding society, and I know our lads will be a big part of that.'[32] I thought it was a magnificent letter, brimming with decency, salience, and bite. A good deed in an anxious summer.

Within a few weeks, however, global events took a truly dispiriting turn. For a few searing weeks both sport and climate change were pushed off the front pages by the fall of Kabul to the Taliban on Sunday 15 August 2021, after twenty years of US and NATO military presence and great efforts towards nation- and civil society-building by international and NGO agencies in Afghanistan. It was, I thought at the time, one of those events that would loom large in our individual and collective memories, and which would impact the calculus of our foreign and defence politics possibly for decades to come.

Five days after Kabul fell, I attempted an initial assessment of its significance. I began by asking:

> Will it scar us in the way the Suez humiliation did [in 1956 and after] as a constant back reference point for (in this case, shared) failure?*
>
> If so, what might the policy consequences mean? Might we well and truly lose what Douglas Hurd called our 'instinct to intervene … We are always looking for different playing fields'? (He said this when we were on a panel together at a meeting of the Cambridge University Land Society in the Travellers' Club on 16 June 2011).[33] We certainly won't be casting our eyes around for fresh mountains on which to display our politico-military prowess for a good while.†
>
> In terms of the public consciousness, those pictures from Kabul Airport of Afghans clinging to the sides of taxiing US transport planes or mothers passing their babies to soldiers over the barbed wire and unable to follow will matter far more than any single paragraph in last March's Integrated Defence and Security Review which hardly anybody will have read.

On the political front, I contrasted the government's conduct with that of Tom Tugendhat, an Afghan veteran, an old friend of mine, and Conservative chairman of the House of Commons Foreign Affairs Select Committee. A few days earlier, Tom had delivered one the great Commons speeches of modern times. His peroration before a chamber, packed for the first time since the

---

* In 1956 the Anglo-French invasion of Egypt, intended to retake the recently nationalised Suez Canal, was halted under intense economic and diplomatic pressure from the United States.

† Interestingly, on this point, Dominic Raab told the Foreign Affairs Select Committee of the House of Commons on 1 September 2021 that 'in the US, domestic support for those kind of interventions has fallen away', adding: 'There is a question of what our polity, our public will be willing to support.' (Patrick Wintour, Heather Stewart, *The Guardian*, 1 September 2021).

pre-Covid period, three days after Kabul fell, was, I thought, quite magnificent: 'That is what defeat looks like; it is when you no longer have the choice of how to help. This does not need to be defeat, but at the moment it damn well feels like it.'[34]

As he sat down, a round of applause, that great rarity in the House of Commons, rippled around the chamber, with the leader of the Opposition, Sir Keir Starmer, joining in.

I drew a contrast in my assessment at the end of that week, on 20 August 2021:

> The picture of helplessness and ineptitude of Johnson and Raab will also linger, reinforcing yet again the impression of a man unfit to be PM presiding over a third-rate Cabinet. Tom Tugendhat *will* be remembered for his heartfelt elegy for the deaths of his friends and the ruin of a policy.

Meanwhile:

> In the wider world, all the wrong people will have been cheering, though both Russia and China will be anxious of a jihadist state in one of the geopolitical hotspots contiguous – or near contiguous – with their borders or those of their client states. The NATO model for out-of-area interventions is deeply tarnished.
>
> Might Kabul 2021 mean that Joe Biden loses his Presidency in November 2024? His denial on 8 July that Kabul 2021 would be anything like Saigon 1975 will run and run and be replayed forever.
>
> The UK, however, will continue to admire its Armed Forces, revere the 457 dead and care about the lives of the injured and the maimed.
>
> If it is to be playing fields no more, we will be a different nation. At the very least, Afghanistan – especially when combined with the memory of the Iraq invasion of 2003 and after – will have changed the mood music in which future policy is made and decisions taken about what to do and what not to do when the

world thrusts another event or enormity upon our attentions. It is easy to call for yet another inquiry – but we need one.

On Saturday 28 August, thirteen days after the fall of Kabul, the last UK civilian evacuation flight left the airport. Nearly 15,000 people had been brought out. Probably another 10,000 were left behind whom the UK wished to evacuate under Operation Pitting. At 3:59 a.m. local time in Kabul on the night of Monday 30 August 2021, the last US soldier to leave, Major General Chris Donahue, commander of the 82nd Airborne Division, was caught by a night-sight infrared camera walking up the ramp into the belly of a huge C-17 transport plane. The twenty-year war was over. British ministers and Whitehall departments squabbled over culpability. The withdrawal left scars of shame and humiliation on the British national psyche that will not heal for a very long time.

The Afghan endgame left the Western allies in disarray. Long-standing patterns of consultation had been ruptured, trust shredded. President Biden's judgement was everywhere questioned. But the biggest of all international co-operation questions – the mitigating and averting of climate change – remained paramount. Its ever-pressing nature affected all the 197 countries spread across the earth's crust.

It was as relentless as the rising sea levels it was precipitating. Some societies had known forever the bounty and cruelty bound up in the giver and taker of life – water. There is a line in Amartya Sen's memoir, *Home in the World*, that captures this perfectly. Writing of 'navigable rivers and the flourishing of civilizations', the Indian economist and Nobel Prize winner offered the example of Bengal: 'Given the traditionally river-centred life of the Bengalis, it is quite natural that social and cultural issues are frequently given some kind of river-based analogy. The river supports human life, sustains it, destroys it and can kill it.'[35]

The capriciousness of water is now bound into everyone's notion of life and society. Only recently has such an understanding come to *all* of us. Water makes life possible. It provides us with great quantities of protein in the form of fish. It permits the transport of goods and raw materials over vast distances. It bathes us. It enabled our rise. It may bring about our fall.

The 'Summary for Policymakers' produced by the UN's Intergovernmental Panel on Climate Change (IPCC) in July 2021 ahead of the COP26 meeting in Glasgow that November is, naturally, replete with the oceanic perils of climate change, albeit in the driest scientific language:

> Global mean sea level has risen faster since 1900 than over any preceding century in at least the last 3000 years (high confidence). The global ocean has warmed faster over the past century than since the last deglacial transition (around 11,000 years ago) (medium confidence) ... Ocean warming accounted for 91% of the heating in the climate system. With land warming, ice loss and atmospheric warming accounting for about 5%, 3%, and 1% respectively (high confidence).[36]

The heat already put into the seas and oceans by human activity since 1750 cannot be removed. Hence the panel's conclusion: 'It is *virtually certain* that global mean sea level will continue to rise over the 21st century.'[37]

The nature and pace of climate change, the science involved in its measurement and prediction, are always complicated and often opaque. For those of us living in the archipelago known as the British Isles, there is one aspect, however, that has captured our anxious imaginings – the Gulf Stream question, or the matter of the 'Atlantic meridional overturn as circulation', which governs the Gulf Stream's flow, as the IPCC's scientists put it.[38]

For many of us, in the part of the brain that stores the geography lessons of our schooldays, the Gulf Stream holds an enduringly vivid place. This great motor of the oceanic system means that our latitudinal position is not dry and cold like that of Labrador in

Canada but moist and mild and altogether easier to live our lives in thanks to the warm water that flows from the Gulf of Mexico (hence its name) north and west until it caresses our shores. The keener geographers among us might just remember being told what happened the last time the Gulf Stream collapsed. Huge torrents rushing down from the melting ice caps and glaciers stretching from the North Pole across all of Canada and halfway down what would later be called the United States shattered the 'thermohaline cycle', as climatologists call it, which 'plunged Europe into a mini ice age for 1,000 years'.[39]

One of my favourite places is a little community garden in the village of St Margaret's Hope on South Ronaldsay in the Orkney Islands. It's about twenty feet above the waters of Scapa Flow. In the middle of it is a tall and proudly flourishing palm tree, the very symbol of the Gulf Stream's bounty. In the late summer and early autumn of 2021, it had become my template for judging the high politics of climate change. What will COP26 do for the Marengo Community Garden and the waterfront beneath it (which already floods quite frequently when the wind is across the Flow hurling the sea high), in the village that is known, fittingly enough, as The Hope? So vast and daunting is the scale of climate change that all of us need something or somewhere to project our fears and hopes onto, to make the subject manageable without diminishing its magnitude.

The key point in the great struggle for the oceanic flows that most affect our islands is about 1,500 miles north-west of the Marengo Garden, across the Atlantic, just south of Iceland. Here the warm, dense, saline waters of the Gulf Stream plunge deep and turn back south, just touching Greenland, then down the Canadian littoral in a vast rotational movement. As a NASA study published in February 2020 put it, the 'delicate Arctic environment ... is now flooded with fresh water, one effect of human-caused climate change'.[40] The trouble is the Gulf Stream is slowing down. The question is: will the Gulf Stream eventually stop?

In one of the most unnerving paragraphs from the IPCC report of Summer 2021, we are invited to peer into a post-Gulf Stream world:

> The Atlantic Meridional Overturning Circulation is *very likely* to weaken over the 21st century for all emissions scenarios. While there is *high confidence* in the 21st century decline, there is only *low confidence* in the magnitude of the trend. There is *medium confidence* that there will not be an abrupt collapse before 2100. If such a collapse were to occur, it would *very likely* cause abrupt shifts in regional weather patterns and water cycle, such as a southward shift in the tropical rain belt, weakening of the African and Asian monsoons and strengthening of the Southern Hemisphere monsoons, and drying in Europe.[41]

For all its coldly clinical language, this paragraph throws a shadow over the Marengo Garden and pretty well everything else.

Wherever you cast your eyes in September 2021, it was hard to find individual or clusters of governments, regional or international organisations, that were coping well with existing problems and difficulties at home and abroad. The prospect of facing such massive dislocations caused by the worst-case scenarios captured in the IPCC's 'Summary for Policymakers' inspires a level of alarm that can all too easily slip into an overwhelming sense of pessimism. You cannot negotiate with a raging glacial meltwater river surging relentlessly beneath the Arctic and Greenland ice caps and pouring its powerful torrent in the direction of the waters of the Gulf Stream coming up from the south for the great showdown off the southern tip of Iceland.

Nature always has the last word. The physics and chemistry of the oceans is oblivious to what George Orwell described as 'the smelly little orthodoxies' of politics.[42] And the world has come increasingly to appreciate that, in the words of the former US Democratic senator for Wisconsin, Gaylord Nelson, 'The economy is a wholly owned subsidiary of the environment, not the other way around.'[43]

Human beings, however, can apply thought, application, and organisation towards mitigating and to a degree averting environmental catastrophe. The climate question is – and will remain – the greatest single weathermaker of our politics and policy for the remainder of the lives of everybody breathing in the world's air, wherever they are, as I write this sentence up the hill from the Marengo Garden. It adds a whole new level of poignancy to the Naval hymn and its call for mercy 'for those in peril on the sea' and the land that girdles it.*

In the early autumn of 2021, the list of those (people, places, and things) in peril was large; the resources (human, political, and financial) to tackle those perils finite. Britain was a land crying out for hope; glory seemed, apart from the wonderful summer of sport we had just experienced, a very distant prospect. Our history, ancient, distant, recent, and instant alike, was weighing heavily upon the kingdom. Our foremost house of government, 10 Downing Street, was placed in the most untrustworthy pair of hands, our parliament mired in the stale cliches and capricious vagaries so disliked by the nation, our public services disdained or scapegoated. And yet, the 2020s contained the capacity to surprise and self-raise. Might these events turn themselves around in the months to come?

Such were my thoughts through an Orkney window as the wind blew and the nights drew in in September 2021.

---

* One of the greatest experiences of my professional life was singing this 30 m down in the waters just north of the Isle of Arran, in a Royal Navy Trafalgar-class submarine in the course of researching *The Silent Deep: The Royal Navy Submarine Service Since 1945*, co-written with James Jinks (London: Allen Lane, 2015).

1

An Autumn of Discontent

Good government depends on good people.

Lord (Gus) O'Donnell, former Cabinet secretary, 16 November 2021[1]

We are all in a very dark place. It is also a sad
day for democracy and parliament.

Sir Lindsay Hoyle, speaker of the House of Commons, Friday 15 October 2021[2]

Seasons of unrest often acquire their own symbols. During the 1978–9 Winter of Discontent, it was the British Salt plant in Middlewich, Cheshire.[3] Once it was picketed, one of the key ingredients of the food processing industry was cut off and the British public swiftly became aware of two things: our increasing reliance on one or two installations for the provision of life's essentials, and the perilous loss of resilience in a society whose supply chains rested increasingly on so-called just-in-time systems of production, distribution and retail.

In the early weeks of the 2021 'autumn of discontent' it was a pair of fertiliser factories – one at Ince in Cheshire, another at Billingham in Teesside – that showed how dangerously reliant the whole country was on one of their by-products, carbon dioxide (CO_2). Some 60 per cent of our CO_2 came from the Ince and Billingham plants, both operated by an American company, CF Fertilisers. Until mid-September 2021, when CF closed down its works because of soaring gas prices, very few people realised just how crucial CO_2 was to the manufacture or safety of so many things (extending food freshness; putting out electrical fires; stunning pigs and chickens before they were slaughtered; converting hydrogen into aviation fuel; keeping food in a good condition during transit).[4]

Symbols are easy to pick up. They obtrude. To a very large degree they suggest themselves. But hoovering up quite what they symbolise – the width and depth of it – is particularly difficult even when one is living through it. So it was in the early autumn of 2021, in that lull between the party-conference season and the House of Commons gathering once more.

On some of the bleaker days, it was as if the familiar shape of the UK had mutated into a petri dish in which a culture of discontentment, resentment, and anxiety seethed and grew. The only relief was the prime minister's uncharacteristic silence. He was off painting in Marbella after a noisy performance at the Conservative Party conference, where he had excelled yet again as the finest exponent in modern times of the politics of the music hall to the rapture of the audience and, one suspects, himself. I have never known a PM who has inhaled so deeply on his self-confected legend.

I tried to capture some of the mood and moment in my diary entry for Wednesday 13 October:

Covid-bereaved families are pushing for the public inquiry to start earlier than next spring.[5]

Number of new Covid cases [42,766] is the worst since mid-July.

The shortage of care home workers is becoming more acute (112,000 people needed).

Reports that China plans to build more coal-fired power stations and hints that it may slow down carbon-emissions plans because of energy crisis after a meeting of its National Energy Commission.[6]

HGV driver shortage and 50,000 container backlog at Felixstowe Docks is causing big shipping companies to divert their vessels to other European ports. Maersk, the Danish freighters (biggest of them all), predicted the problem would last until the new year.[7]

Jim Radcliffe (CEO of INEOS)* tells Robert Peston [of ITN] that the UK could run out of gas this winter if the weather's bad (we only have 10 days' worth in storage). Two more energy companies have gone bust.

The EU produces its proposals for Northern Ireland trade. Dramatic reduction in paperwork. Free flow for medicines and chilled meat. Jeffrey Donaldson [leader of the Democratic Unionist Party] says this still falls far short of what is needed.

Leo Varadkar [then the former Taoiseach and a crucial figure in the negotiation of the Brexit Northern Ireland Protocol] says if the UK reneges on the NI Protocol he would warn other countries not to make deals with the UK as Britain would have become a country that does not keep its promises.

Dominic Cummings adds his customary sulphur in the following tweet (which reinforces Varadkar's point). It starts with a whiff of *coup d'étatism*:

'We took over a party on ~10%, worst constitutional crisis in century, much of deep state angling for BINO [Brexit in name only] or 2REF [second referendum]. So we wriggled thro with best option we cd & intended to get [Johnson] to ditch bits we didn't like after whacking Corbyn [in a general election]. We prioritised … For all the cant about international law, a/ states break it every week, b/ the idea it's the epitome of morality is low grade student politics pushed by lawyers/officials to constrain politics they oppose.'[8]

So much for international law! So much for treaties mattering! DC is suggesting that going back on the NI Protocol was the plan all along – even if it meant removing ourselves from the list of rule-of-law states. What kind of image does DC have of the country

---

* A huge manufacturing conglomerate.

that nurtured him? What kind of international reputation does he wish us to have?

Cummings' Tweets encapsulate the unnerving features of the autumn of discontent: the ever-lurking presence of Covid; the needs of the care sector; the shortage of trucks; the fuel crisis; the fragility of the UK's just-in-time manufacturing, delivering, and retailing arrangements; the continuing curse of Brexit; the government's appetite for behaving like a rogue state; the worries about real change on the part of the world's polluter nations. But there were plenty more, some of which, I feared, would only become apparent later. An age of anxiety is always marked by a sense of anticipatory pessimism – even on the part of natural optimists like myself. Partly it was because there was still so much to absorb since March 2020 when Covid first fell upon us.

For example, my diary entry about the Covid-bereaved reflected part of the impact earlier in the week of perhaps the most impressive and substantial House of Commons select committee reports of modern times, *Coronavirus: Lessons Learned to Date*.[9] It was published on 12 October, just a few days after a freedom-of-information request had caused Public Health England to release the February 2016 report on Exercise Alice, a pandemic modelling exercise that sought to examine the readiness and resilience 'to respond to a large-scale outbreak of MERS [Middle East respiratory syndrome]-CoV in England'.[10] Alice declared that the 'level and use of personal protective equipment (PPE) was central to the exercise dialogue and considered of crucial importance for front line staff'.[11]*

The select committee concluded that the pre-planning had been too narrow and inflexible.[12] One of its key recommendations was improved and better resourced contingency planning 'for future

---

* Exercise Alice was tasked 'to explore the compatibility for contact tracing and quarantining of possible MERS-CoV cases' and it 'identified 12 specific actions and four key themes ... These included quarantine versus self-isolation and the clarity required about the options; PPE level ... and effective proportional communications'.

risks and emergencies'.[13] It also laid out 'six key areas' for the government's public inquiry to examine how it sets about its task:

> The country's preparedness for a pandemic; the use of non-pharmaceutical interventions such as border controls, social distancing and lockdowns to control the pandemic; the use of test and trace and isolate strategies; the impact of the pandemic on social care; the impact of the pandemic on specific communities; and the procurement and roll-out of Covid-19 vaccines.[14]

Combined with the steadily rising number of new daily cases, publication of the select-committee report added to the sense of multiple fragilities in the UK of autumn 2021.

Three days later, tragedy struck in a terrible fashion with the stabbing to death of Sir David Amess MP in Leigh-on-Sea while he was holding a constituency surgery in his seat of Southend West. Sir David was one of those rare politicians who combine very strong opinions with a deep affability that aroused affection right across the benches of the House of Commons. This was evident the following Monday when MPs gathered to pay tribute in the Chamber and to pray across the road in St Margaret's, Westminster.

The Economist's 'Bagehot' columnist reported:

> They told stories about the man with the widest grin in Westminster: how this lifelong Roman Catholic had once got the Pope to bless a boiled sweet by mistake and how this inveterate campaigner for city status for Southend deluged the authorities with proof of the place's worthiness, such as the fact that it held the world record for the number of triangles played simultaneously.[15]

(The prime minister announced that the Queen had approved city status for the jewel of the Thames estuary during his tribute to his slain colleague. A nice touch.) A twenty-five-year-old Somali Britain, Ali Harbi Ali, had been arrested at the scene. Harbi Ali was later sentenced to a whole-life term in prison after being found guilty of Sir David's murder.

It brought back memories of June 2016, when another much-loved MP, Jo Cox, had been murdered by a neo-Nazi on her way to holding a surgery in her Yorkshire constituency of Batley and Spen, which she held for Labour. Once again the overall security of our politicians and the prized personal accessibility of MPs for constituents was called into question. Sir Lindsay Hoyle and the home secretary, Priti Patel, announced there would be a review. There was much talk of the sheer nastiness of the early 2020s in public and political life and the daily torrent of venomous tweets that MPs, especially women politicians, receive, as well as the dangers of extremism generally.

Between the select committee report on Covid lessons learned and the assassination of David Amess, another significant 'interim' assessment was made public – this one into the performance of the British state under the stress of pandemic and the lessons for both the recovery period and any future emergencies that might befall us. It was delivered in the form of a lecture at the University of Newcastle by Dr Simon Case, the cabinet secretary.[16] Its significance became even more apparent two weeks later when the chancellor, Rishi Sunak, unveiled a Budget brimming with spending plans for a post-pandemic interventionist state that his (Sunak's) deputy, chief secretary to the Treasury, Simon Clarke, described as 'a philosophical shift' for the Conservative Party.[17]

Dr Case told his Newcastle audience that the pandemic and the recovery to come gave Whitehall a real chance 'to renew and rewire government'. He was haunted by the 'missed opportunity' to reform after the Second World War (kindly referring to a chapter with that title in my 1989 study, *Whitehall*):[18]

The Government had corralled the nation's best talents for the war effort: scientists, engineers, mechanics, linguists, cryptographers – yes, even historians – whomever was necessary. After victory, we could have applied their specialist skills, their expertise and knowledge, to rebuild the country. Instead, they were encouraged to disperse. There was never a formal examination into how the state as a whole had performed in the war. Which meant no one realised just how much government had been boosted by this rapid infusion of external expertise.

In order to 'avoid the curse of the "Missed Opportunity"', he declared, we 'must make sure that in the next five years we learn the lessons of the pandemic and we seize the opportunities to bank our wins and fix our weaknesses'.[19] The areas he stressed as in need of improvement included better decision-taking based on enhanced data collection and skills; the need to make the state more resilient in future emergencies; improved training for civil servants; a boosted inward flow of people from the private sector; an invigoration of relationships with local government, all infused with the ethos of trust-creating 'impartial advice ... and in the truth we speak unto power. We jeopardise this at our peril, for reputations can be lost easier and faster than ever they are won'. The Civil Service, he concluded, 'has given its all during the course of the pandemic, yet must now summon its strength for another great push as we rebuild and reshape the country'. [20]

The Newcastle lecture, I thought, was Simon Case's swift and streamlined account of why Whitehall was not reformed after the Second World War,[21] and also of the Fulton Report of 1968, the last time there had been a major inquiry into the Civil Service (which had much to say about the greater use of experts, improved decision-making and training).[22] Yet amidst the anxieties and news flurries of the autumn of discontent, it attracted virtually no public attention.

Unlike the 'big state' implications of the Budget a fortnight after. It was bound to be a touchstone Budget – one that indicated how much of the Covid-stimulated deployment of money and powers might, or should, persist once the viral crisis had eased – in short, what a new stable political economy for the early 2020s would look like. As we listened to Rishi Sunak delivering it, we had no idea about the kind of fourth-wave pandemic about to hit or the bizarre concatenation of events – old and new – that would make the prime minister's personal autumn of discontent so ravaging for his premiership, for his party and for the public's trust in politicians more generally.

When I first reported on Whitehall as a young journalist in the mid-to-late 1970s, Budgets were sacred things, secret until the moment the chancellor was on his feet divulging the details to a packed House of Commons. Now, they trickle out in a series of pre-Budget leaks, part, one suspects, of some clever-Dick media strategy for creating a flow of good-news stories. The October 2021 Budget was an absolute classic of this kind of fiscal foreplay, snippets of which I recorded in my diary:

SATURDAY 23 OCTOBER
Another £500m for young families
£6.9bn for transport in the English City/Regions …

SUNDAY 24 OCTOBER
Another £20bn for research, skills, and training …

MONDAY 25 OCTOBER
National Living Wage is to rise by 6.6%
NHS will receive £5.9bn to tackle its backlog …

TUESDAY 26 OCTOBER
Public sector wage freeze will end next spring …

WEDNESDAY 27 OCTOBER.
The actual Budget and Comprehensive Spending Review – at last!
Was it one of the 'signature' Budgets of the postwar years? It was certainly intended to be.

I attempted to capture the Budget 'in flight':

BIG PICTURE
Based on revised forecasts of faster growth (6.5% this year rather than the 4% predicted by the Office for Budget Responsibility [OBR] in March), less unemployment and a swifter recovery, HMG [Her Majesty's Government] goes for spending now before growth falls back to 1.3% from 1.5% in 3 years' time. And so, the Chancellor says, the tax-cutting can begin.

He portrayed it as an optimistic Budget and so it is. That forecast could turn out to be wishful thinking. It reminds me of Harold Wilson's Labour government in the mid-1960s behaving as if it *had* achieved the 4% growth planned when it was, in fact, an out-turn of 2.5%. Overall tax burden now higher than at any time since the last days of the Attlee government.

Sunak says the Budget is intended to mark the beginning 'of a new age of optimism' built on a 'higher wage, higher productivity' economy.

This last has been the cry of every chancellor of the exchequer in the years since 1945. After the big picture:

THE HEADLINES
- 2 m households will benefit from £2.2 bn alteration to Universal Credit 'tapering' for those in work (but nothing for those recipients who are unemployed.
- Sunak promises real-term rises for 'every single area' of the public service.
- £2 bn of extra funding for schools in England.
- International aid to return to 0.7% of GDP by 2024.
- Borrowing in 2020–21 estimated at £319 bn (15.2% of GDP).
- Sunak says it will fall to 7.9% in the current financial year and to 3.3% next year.
- £1.8 bn for Covid education recovery.

- OBR forecasts public spending will grow from 39.8% of GDP pre-Covid to 41.6% by 2026–7. Tax will rise from 33.5% of GDP to 36.2% [in the same period].

At the end of his speech, Sunak declared himself to be a low-tax/small-state man, which sat rather oddly with all that had gone before and what his chief secretary had to say.

On the economic 'scarring' of Covid, the OBR predicted it would leave the UK economy 2 per cent below its pre-2020 GDP growth trend. It expected the economy to reach pre-Covid levels by the end of the year. It lowered its unemployment forecast from 12 per cent to 5.2 per cent and predicted 4 per cent inflation the following year (it was 3.1 per cent in September).

Paul Johnson, the highly respected director of the Institute for Fiscal Studies, provided, I thought, a necessary corrective to the level of optimism with which Sunak had filled his pen when writing his Budget: 'What the OBR giveth the OBR is perfectly capable of taking away at the next fiscal event ... Rising inflation and rising taxes offset higher earnings and employment. Average earners can expect their real incomes to fall next year.'[23] (Johnson told the BBC *Six O'Clock News* the following day that the UK could be 13 per cent worse off next year because of tax rises and higher inflation.)

The Budget of 27 October 2021 *did*, at the time, appear to be a benchmark document in the modern history of the Conservative Party. Michael Portillo, himself a former chief secretary to the Treasury, bluntly told *Times Radio* the following day that it was 'not Conservative' and presented the party with 'an identity crisis ... This is certainly not Conservative philosophy. This is something quite different.'[24]

A promising debate about quite what this new philosophy might be was cut off by two things: the range of rather greater questions posed by COP26, which began to assemble in Glasgow a few days later, and the more pressing question of Boris Johnson's character and judgement as the Owen Paterson affair began to make political

weather. On 26 October 2021 Owen Paterson, Conservative MP
for North Shropshire, prominent and longstanding Brexiteer and
former Cabinet minister, was found in a unanimous report from
the all-party House of Commons Committee on Standards to have
used his position as an MP to further the interests of Randox, a
clinical diagnostics company, and the food manufacturer Lynn's
Country Foods, to whom he was a paid consultant.[25] The committee recommended that he be 'suspended from the service of the
House for 30 sitting days'.[26]

Normally, the House votes through the Standards Committee's
findings. Mr Paterson claimed its report was flawed as he had not
been able to turn to certain witnesses for his defence. He determined to fight his corner in the Chamber rather than just accept his
penalty. He had some support for this action and, especially, Boris
Johnson decided to add his.

Not only would the Conservative's business managers whip in
favour of Paterson's amendment, but they would also, as a government, press for a reshaping of the Standards Committee and its supporting apparatus.

On Wednesday 3 November this duly happened, as I noted in
my diary:

> Owen Paterson's suspension is paused after a Commons
> vote (*shamefully* whipped by the government) sets up a new
> committee to examine standards procedure. Labour, Lib Dems
> and SNP refuse to sit on it. Chris Bryant [Labour MP for Rhondda],
> who chairs the Standards Committee, says it will look to the
> public as if 'we are marking our own homework' ... It is a *huge*
> misjudgement. Johnson has a habit of trying to just sweep aside
> any convention, procedure or institution that gets in his or his
> government's way. It will be his undoing.

The public reaction was one of anger. A YouGov poll taken the
following evening showed that the Conservatives' lead had fallen

by three points (Conservatives: 36; Labour: 35),[27] despite a government U-turn in the meantime. In an instant, it had reopened the Barnard Castle scandal (involving the behaviour of Dominic Cummings and Johnson's reaction to it in April/May 2020), and the claim that it was one law for them and quite another for the rest of us.

As for the U-turn, the morning after the whipped Conservative vote, I recorded how Jacob Rees-Mogg, leader of the House,

> says it's because the other political parties will not take part in the proposed new committee. Instead there will be another vote and an emergency debate. Paterson resigns his North Shropshire seat. At the request of his children he will leave 'the cruel world of politics'.
>
> This is a signature crisis for the government: chaos and an inability to think things through in No.10; the PM's complete lack of feel for propriety and proper procedure. The willingness of the supine on his own backbenches when summoned to do his bidding. But, whatever Paterson has or has not done, his resignation is a reminder of the tragedy that shadows the whole affair – the loss of his wife, Rose.*

That same day, Jonathan Evans (Lord Evans of Weardale), former director general of MI5, now a crossbench peer and chairman of the Committee on Standards in Public Life, delivered a stinging rebuke at the Institute for Government:

> Nobody should be able to make their own judgements on their own case ... I do think that we should not take for granted either the fact that this country has relatively low levels of corruption or our international reputation, because it's easy to say we've always had a good reputation. Well, we've had a good reputation

---

* She had died by suicide in June 2020.

because of the decisions that have been made. It's not inherent in the nature of the country that we will not be corrupt. We could slip into being a corrupt country, and that's why we need to be vigilant around these issues. It's also quite possible we could slip in terms of international perceptions of us.[28]

It is unusual for a regulator to speak out in such strong terms. But the highly respected Lord Evans believes that the sustenance of ethical standards and the maintenance of proper procedures are very much part of defending the realm (the motto of his old service).[29]

Two days later, Sir John Major – who was prime minister at another time of anxiety about 'sleaze', and who in 1994 set up the Committee on Standards in Public Life to be what he called an 'ethical workshop'[30] – weighed into the debate. For some years Sir John had shown a sense of timing in his rare (but always astute) public interventions almost worthy of his great cricketing hero, Sir Jack Hobbs.

Speaking to Nick Robinson on the *Today* programme on Saturday 6 November, Sir John described some of Johnson's actions as prime minister as 'un-Conservative'. My note on his remarks ran like this:

The Government was 'politically corrupt' in the way it had treated Parliament. There is a general whiff of 'We are the masters now' about their behaviour.*

It has the effect of trashing the reputation of Parliament.

It has to stop; it has to stop soon.[31]

---

* This is a line familiar to those of my generation and older. It was used by Attlee's attorney general, Sir Hartley Shawcross, though usually misquoted. What Sir Hartley actually said in 1946 was: 'We are the masters at the moment.'

A poll in *The Observer* the following day suggested public opinion was with Major and Evans. It recorded a fall in Johnson's personal approval rating from -16 the previous week to -20, his lowest ever.[32]

On Monday 8 November, Johnson absented himself from the Commons emergency debate on Paterson and the Standards Committee Report (he was visiting a hospital in the North East but was back in London in time to take part if he had chosen to). Instead, the Cabinet Office minister Steve Barclay had to take the flak in the Chamber. He expressed the government's 'regret' for the 'mistake' of having 'conflated' the Paterson case with the need to change the system. Sir Peter Bottomley, the longest-serving MP and therefore 'father of the House', said the system did not need changing. Sir Keir Starmer accused Johnson of 'running scared'. Sir Lindsay Hoyle concluded with a plea to find a way forward.[33] So it was.

There were more to come. Within a few days, questions arose about MPs' second jobs when a video emerged of the former attorney general Sir Geoffrey Cox apparently using his Westminster office to conduct private legal work.[34]

The public mood continued to shift against Boris Johnson and his party. On Saturday 13 November, I noted:

This morning's *Daily Mail* has what is usually called 'a shock poll'. Savanta ComRes [the market research consultancy] indicates:

LAB   40%
CONS   34%

Last week it was:
CONS   38%
LAB   35%[35]

The 'sleaze' is biting. If those figures are (a) accurate and (b) turn out to be sustained, the Paterson affair plus Cox and the general aftermath really will have engineered a significant shift in political mood.

The Times' YouGov poll reinforces this impression showing that two-thirds of voters see the Conservatives as 'very sleazy' though the two parties remain neck and neck at 35 each; some 39% believe Johnson is more corrupt than previous prime ministers.[36]

An opinion poll in *The Observer* the following day showed 47 per cent thinking him corrupt and 22 per cent 'honest'.[37]

On Tuesday 16 November, the great dreadnoughts of the British system of government, all five surviving former Cabinet secretaries, slipped from their moorings in the House of Lords and put out to sea once more. The roar of their formidable fifteen-inch guns shook the letters page of *The Times*. The target of Lords Butler, Wilson of Dinton, Turnbull, O'Donnell, and Sedwill was unidentified but unmistakeable. 'To ensure public confidence in the integrity of our public life', they wrote, 'there is an urgent need to put the key standards bodies, in particular the Commissioner for Public Appointments and the Independent Adviser on Ministerial Interests, on to a statutory basis.'[38] When talking about this letter on that morning's *Today* programme, Gus O'Donnell pithily updated the 'good chap' theory of government [39] with his dictum, 'Good government depends on good people'.

Tuesday 16 November was to be a day of letters. As we absorbed the words of the ancients of the Whitehall tribe, the prime minister wrote another one to the speaker of the House of Commons proposing a ban on MPs being paid for consultancy work and the giving of strategic advice.[40] Later that day, in the Chamber, during the emergency debate on the Paterson case and the Standards Committee, Theresa May declared: 'The attempt by right hon. and hon. members of this House, aided and abetted by the Government under cover of reform of the process, effectively to clear his name was misplaced, ill-judged and just plain wrong.'[41]

The prime minister realised he was outgunned. There were

angry exchanges at Prime Minister's Questions on 17 November. The speaker intervened on both Johnson and Starmer, telling the former pointedly: 'You may be the prime minister of this country, but in this House I am in charge.'[42] Of the Paterson affair, the prime minister did admit: 'It was a mistake and it was my mistake.'[43] That evening, at the weekly meeting of the 1922 Committee, he said he had 'crashed the car'.[44]

A train was about to crash, metaphorically, too – the high-speed one from London to the Midlands and the North. On 16 November, reports began to circulate that its Sheffield/Leeds branch was going to be scrapped. Two days later this was confirmed when the government published its *Integrated Rail Plan [IRP] for the North and the Midlands*.[45] The Treasury, ever searching for savings, had prevailed. The eastern limb of HS2 would now not be built, arousing fury in West Yorkshire, and widening once more the (never closed) sense of a North/South divide. 'We feel completely and utterly let down,' said Tracy Brabin, the mayor of West Yorkshire.*[46] And so they have been, despite the improvements announced for trans-Pennine routes, because they will not cover as much of the Manchester–Leeds lines as expected.

Johnson went to Selby in Yorkshire to defend his rail plan. There, on 18 November, in his Network Rail high-vis rig, he gave an interview to Krishnan Guru-Murthy of Channel 4 News (on behalf of the journalists' pool), gets ratty and burbly (repeatedly telling KGM: 'You're talking rubbish'). He also refuses to apologise for the Paterson affair.[47] That day I ask in my diary: 'Has Johnson reached a point of no return? Everything he touches turns to manure'.

It did so again – spectacularly, weirdly, and undeniably – in

---

* This sense of frustration and disappointment barely dissipated over the subsequent year. On the first anniversary of the launch of the IRP, Brabin and Oliver Coppard, the newly elected mayor of South Yorkshire, released a joint statement bemoaning the paucity of its ambition and citing its lack of progress. Coppard was particularly scathing: 'To grow our economy, create good jobs and connect our cities, towns, and villages, Yorkshire needs the full fat Northern Powerhouse Rail, not the semi-skimmed version.'

Newcastle but four days later. It was almost as if travelling north of the Home Counties unhinged him. The day before, Andrew Marr, when announcing he was to leave the BBC, declared: 'As a lifelong political hack, I now feel that we should spend less time on the distracting national puppet show.'[48]

Johnson's performance at the Confederation of British Industry's annual conference at the Port of Tyne saw him surpass the puppet show in what I described in my diary as

> one of the most bizarre and inadequate speeches in the modern history of the premiership. It will be remembered forever as his 'Peppa Pig' speech. He devoted one quarter of his address to what *The Times'* first leader writer called 'a bizarre riff' on Peppa Pig World, a theme park in Hampshire that Mr Johnson had visited the day before and which he recommended as 'his kind of place'.

The leader article went on: 'He wistfully recalled his time as motoring correspondent for *GQ Magazine*, imitating car noises to emphasize whatever point he was trying to make. He likened himself to Moses bringing down his ten-point green energy plan from Mount Sinai. At one point he lost his thread completely, mumbling "forgive me" as he fumbled with his pages.'[49] Asked by a reporter after his speech if he was all right, the prime minister replied: 'I thought it went over well.' That evening, after watching this disaster of a performance unfold on television, I wondered if he *was* unwell: 'He's plainly very tired. Even the insensitive suffer from strain. The rambling. The even thinner grasp of detail, I wonder ... The accumulation of gaffes and follies and misjudgements could be tipping his backbenchers into regarding him as an electoral liability. If it is – then he's in real trouble.' We would soon see. Owen Paterson's resignation had triggered a by-election in North Shropshire. Was there the sound of a clock ticking Oswestry way?

Yet another former leader of the Conservative Party, William Hague, added his thoughts on the Johnson malaise in his weekly column in *The Times*, calling for Johnson 'to make Cabinet government operate effectively. The prime minister could benefit from having a group of senior colleagues whom he meets every day. They ought to be discussing their whole strategy together frankly'.[50] The problem was with his set of ministers – which ones would add value and judgement? Probably only Sunak. More to the point, Johnson was an 'ego PM' of the highest order, not a collective one. Boris Johnson and the British constitution simply do not fit. I wonder if he was, deep down, aware of this. The day after his 'Peppa Pig' moment, an old Conservative-Cabinet-minister friend of mine from years back, always a shrewd judge of character, thought he *had* come to realise this – that his kind of cleverness did not work.[51]

The engine room of the British version of Cabinet government – the Civil Service – found itself very much in the frame that morning. Aptly enough, it was in *The Times*' 'Thunderer' column that Dame Kate Bingham, heroine of the Covid vaccine procurement, let rip her lightning flash of criticism. 'Across government,' she wrote,

> there is a devastating lack of skills and experience in science, industry and manufacturing ... This would not matter if we had senior civil servants with scientific and technical understanding needed to be operationally effective. But we don't ... Why is this important? Because if you lack scientific knowledge, then you cannot make the right decisions about science and medicine.[52]

I agree with every word of that – as with her strictures on foresight and contingency planning.

'The machinery of government,' she continued, 'is dominated by process, rather than outcome, causing delay and inertia.' We need, she argued, 'a peacetime capability for dealing with major healthcare threats. These are just as serious – and potentially fatal – as national security and defence yet they receive a fraction of the level of government investment and attention.'[53]

'Have we found the chair for a new Fulton inquiry?'* I wondered in my diary – a feeling reinforced a few days later when Simon Case accepted the thrust of her argument in a letter to *The Times*: 'Dame Kate Bingham is correct in her assessment of the lack of skills and experience in science, industry and manufacturing across government ... The government's chief scientific adviser, Sir Patrick Vallance, is working to bring in science and engineering expertise at all levels.'[54]

For all the long-term importance of the Cabinet secretary's theme, For all the long-term importance of the Cabinet secretary's theme, Friday 26 November 2021 will, as my diary records, be remembered not for that but for this:

> A new word has entered the Covid lexicon – OMICRON – the name the WHO [World Health Organization] has given to B.1.1.529, the emerging, highly transmissible strain from southern Africa. It seems to be mutating fast and it's on its travels – it has reached Hong Kong, Israel, and Belgium. Scientists say it will take 2 to 3 weeks to evaluate it fully. Airlines are cancelling flights from southern Africa. Stock markets fell around the world. Will the vaccines prove to be effective against it when it strikes a highly immunised country?

Another immediate question was posed by the all too understandable 'not again' feeling everyone felt. Chief medical adviser Chris Whitty spoke of the possibility of 'behavioural fatigue'. He told a meeting of the Local Government Association:

> My greatest worry at the moment is that if we need to do something more muscular, at some point, whether it is for the current new variant or at some later stage, can we still take the people

---

* The Fulton Committee on the Civil Service sat between 1966 and 1968. It also stressed the need for more specialisation in the senior Civil Service.

with us? ... [We will] provided we're clear to people what the logic is and provided they feel that we're being entirely straight with them as to all the data and the knowns and unknowns.[55]

Even though a fourth wave of Covid had been widely anticipated, there was still an element of fear that this new variant would harm us in new and different ways, and at a faster pace.

SATURDAY 27 NOVEMBER 2021
A day of foreboding about OMICRON. Johnson, flanked by Whitty and Vallance, announces 'temporary and precautionary measures ... to slow [the seeding and] the spread', which will be reviewed in 3 weeks' time.[56] They are:

- Mask-wearing in shops and on public transport.
- All OMICRON contacts to isolate for 10 days.
- PCR test for all travellers arriving in the UK.
- The gap between second and third vaccinations will be reduced.

During Q and A, Whitty says OMICRON has 'quite extensive mutations' on its spike protein. Vallance explains that it is the combination of transmissibility and the mutations that is causing concern. The PM says its vaccination programme puts the UK in a strong position: 'This Christmas will be considerably better than the last one.'[57]

TUESDAY 30 NOVEMBER 2021
OMICRON, over the space of just a few days, has come to dominate our anxieties and our politics. Johnson says, 'We're going to throw everything at it.' By this he means that, above all, a huge booster programme mobilising the NHS and pharmacies to provide booster jabs – 25 to 40 m of them – for everyone by the end of January. 400 members of the military will join NHS volunteers in

the big push … The House of Commons votes for the government's measures (majorities of 395 and 411). The sense of the precarious has risen markedly (it had never gone away – but it had faded).

On 6 December, at the Blavatnik School of Government at Oxford University, Dame Sarah Gilbert, Said professor of vaccinology at the university's Jenner Institute and leader of the team that developed the AstraZeneca vaccine, delivered a superb BBC Richard Dimbleby Lecture on the theme of 'humanity against the viruses'. 'This pandemic is not done with us,' she said, while going on to warn that 'the next one could be worse. It could be more contagious, more lethal, or both.'

Dame Sarah concluded on an optimistic note:

Over the last two painful years, as we struggled to respond, we made discoveries that will be important for decades to come. *Scientific* discoveries that I hope a new generation, inspired by what science can do, will build on to achieve amazing, previously unimaginable things. Just as we built on what had come before. But perhaps above all, as we turn our attack back to climate change, poverty, war, and other problems that never went away, what we discovered was what we can do when we understand our goal, and really put our minds to achieving it.[58]

Scratchy politics-as-usual, of course, had never gone away either. It never does. But it was about to enter an intense and peculiar phase mixing the pandemic, *last* year's Christmas parties in Downing Street, and the Johnson character question.

At Prime Minister's Questions on 1 December, there was a row about whether or not a party was held in No. 10 on 18 December 2020. The following day, the Conservatives held Bexley and Sidcup in London's south-east suburbs following the death of the respected Cabinet minister James Brokenshire, albeit with a reduced majority and a ten-point swing to Labour since the 2019 general election.

The public mood was already soured enough. A YouGov poll in *The Observer* on Sunday 5 December suggested that only 5 per cent of the public believed that MPs work for the public good. It was part of a study undertaken by the Institute of Public Policy Research which indicated that there had been a sharp fall in public esteem of the political class generally since the Paterson affair broke.[59]

Worse was to follow, thanks to one of the most dramatic – and, possibly, most politically significant – leaks of modern times. In my diary for Tuesday 7 December, I tried to capture how it broke and how it felt as the initial aftershock spread:

> The ITN 6:30 has a dramatic scoop – a 'smoking film' of a dummy press conference held on 22 December 2020 as part of Allegra Stratton's* preparation of the job-that-never-was as the PM's daily, on-the-record press spokesman. She is asked by Ed Oldroyd[†] about the 18 DEC party. Laughing and joking, they [or, rather, she] try [tries] to explain it away as 'a business meeting' which was not 'socially distanced' and involved wine and cheese.
>
> It struck me as a deadly combination of lying and laughing. Robert Peston describes it as 'very dangerous ... making light of important rules being broken'.
>
> On the BBC Ten No. 10 were still denying that there was a party.

Johnson persisted with the there-was-no-party line at Prime Minister's Questions the following day, telling the Commons that he had asked Simon Case to investigate. He appeared to dump the blame on Allegra Stratton with not a trace of chivalry. Starmer was highly effective in his attack, somehow managing to mobilise the Queen (the care she had shown to keep to the rules at Prince Philip's funeral) and the comedians Ant and Dec (who had referred to

---

* Formerly a *Guardian* and *Newsnight* political correspondent.
† One of the prime minister's special advisers.

the party in the previous night's episode of *I'm a Celebrity... Get Me Out of Here!* in Gwrych Castle) to buttress his case.

Would this be yet another episode in a series of Boris-will-be-Boris incidents that could somehow be swept aside? I thought not, as I put it in my diary on 8 December:

> In the afternoon, Stratton resigns tearfully and apologetically reading a statement outside her North London home: 'I will regret my remarks for the rest of my days.'
>
> I think this may be the defining moment in the Johnson premiership. It is a class apart from all the multiple ghastlinesses that have gone before.

Meanwhile, there was a worsening pandemic to be dealt with. Just after six, the prime minister took to the podium, flanked by Whitty and Vallance, to announce the introduction of Plan B after receiving scientific and medical advice that the UK may face one million Omicron infections by the end of December and up to 2,000 hospitalisations a day. Johnson spoke of 'the remorseless logic of exponential growth'.[60] From the following Monday, we all had to work from home once more if possible. Face masks were back in public places. Covid passports would be required in a week's time in theatres and sporting events involving more than 500 people.

The Christmas-party story was taking on a life of its own, descending into extraordinary detail about what should be construed as a 'party' and what should not. Who was advising Johnson on what had taken place, assuring him it wasn't a 'party'? Was it Jack Doyle – the very man who was now putting out the 'line' as the prime minister's official spokesman? Into this increasingly bizarre set of questions, the 'flat refurbishment' story obtruded once more.

The Electoral Commission investigation had been following the money trail and the electronic traffic. It turned up WhatsApp messages between Johnson and Lord Brownlow, a Conservative Party donor who had contributed £58,000 to help with the refurbishment costs of the prime minister's flat, 'at a time when Johnson previously claimed he did not know the source of the money'.[61] Christopher Geidt, the prime minister's Independent Adviser on Ministers' Interests, asked for – and received – copies of those communications. The question was: had the prime minister inadvertently misled him on this during the course of the initial investigation and would the new material change Lord Geidt's earlier conclusion that Johnson had not breached the Ministerial Code?

On Thursday 9 December, I attempted an assessment of the threat Johnson's multiple woes presented to the survival of his premiership:

> The vectors of forces criss-crossing the floor of the H of C Chamber will be decisive *if* one of the many alleged instances of knowingly misleading the House finally sticks.
>
> It could be the 18 DEC party. Yesterday, it turned out it might be the refurbishment of the PM's flat as the Electoral Commission placed a £14,000 fine on the Conservative Party for less than full disclosure of the money trail. Its findings reveal that Johnson WhatsApped Lord Brownlow about it and that Christopher Geidt was not made aware of this. Tomorrow's papers are speculating that C is considering resigning as the PM's Adviser on the Ministerial Code.
>
> The question is, would Johnson, who is a stranger to decent behaviour, actually *do* the decent thing and go and see the Queen to tell her of his intention to resign if he is shown to have knowingly misled Parliament? Would Graham Brady and the 22 Executive Committee going to see him be enough? The relevant section of the Ministerial Code captures a convention; it does not express a law. In Johnson's scrambled mind, ego will, I suspect, always trump convention or any fragment of the 'good chaps' theory of government, even a part so central as this …

Public opinion continued to move against Johnson. A YouGov

poll published on 10 December put Labour on 37 per cent and the Conservatives on 33 per cent; 61 per cent said the Allegra Stratton video made them feel angry.[62] Two days later, polling data in *The Observer* showed a nine-point lead for Labour (41 per cent to 32 per cent) and that Johnson's personal rating stood at -35 per cent.[63] Downing Street – very sensibly – cancelled its 2021 Christmas party.

Omicron worries threw an ever longer forward shadow over Christmas. On 10 December, Professor Jason Leitch, Scotland's drily fluent Director of Public Health, declared: 'The virus doesn't have a calendar like you and I do.'

Two days later, on 12 December, a grave and tired-looking prime minister broadcast to the nation from No. 10 at 8 p.m.: 'I am afraid we are now facing an emergency ... there is a tidal wave of Omicron coming.'[64]

He went on to describe the government's 'Omicron Emergency Booster National Mission'. The booster programme was to be brought forward by a month so that every adult could be boosted by the end of December. The NHS began to crank up to deliver a million boosters a day with the help of the military.

The 'party' question took another twist. That morning, *The Sunday Mirror* ran a photograph of Johnson apparently hosting a quiz in Downing Street in December 2020. Down it went on to Simon Case's list of items to be investigated.

The country may have been feeling 'compliance fatigue' but it wasn't acting upon it. The day after Johnson's 'tidal wave' broadcast, working from home was up and travel was down. The roads were noticeably quieter. Network Rail reported a 20 per cent drop in footfall at its stations in London and Manchester. Starmer, replying to Johnson's broadcast, said: 'Let's pull together now and do the right thing once more.'

But resistance to Johnson's Omicron plan was rising on his own backbenches, and expressed itself in a series of Commons votes on the evening of Tuesday 14 December. The government carried the day but only with the help of Labour votes. On Covid passports, 101 Conservative MPs voted against – a remarkable rebellion by any standards, which put a serious dent in Johnson's authority.

It struck me that at least three groups were in play among the body of dissident Conservative backbenchers: those who thought the scientists were wrong about the beneficial impact of such passports; those whose libertarianism could not allow for such an affront to our freedoms; and those who, for a variety of reasons, simply wished to biff the prime minister.

It was to be a 'week of the political daggers' for Johnson. There had been signs that some of the people of Oswestry and its environs might be contemplating a tactical vote in the coming by-election. They were. On Thursday 16 December, Boris was no longer Shropshire's lad.

By the time the result came through I was on South Ronaldsay. I reached for the diary:

FRIDAY 17 DECEMBER 2021. ST. MARGARET'S HOPE
8:07 a.m.
Writing this as a pink Orkney dawn slips over the hill from the East after watching the big ferry creep into the Flow to the West not long before 8:00 a.m. while I was still absorbing the glow from 500 miles or so to the south in North Shropshire where the Lib Dems have replaced a 23,000 Conservative majority in the 2019 general election with a nearly 6,000-vote majority of their own – except that it isn't just theirs; in part, it's a reflection of a widespread detestation of Boris Johnson and what his party has become under his stewardship.

It's a great relief that the by-election suggests that the electorate *won't* succumb to a resigned, if regretful, feeling that this is just the way Johnson is and what politics generally has become. We're still shockable by bad behaviour. I've been celebrating with hot tea and a Tunnock's bar (there's euphoria for you)...

Here is the electoral arithmetic:

LD	17,957 (47.22%)
CON	12,032 (31.64%)
LAB	3,686 (9.69%)
TURNOUT	46.2%

34% swing from CON to LIB DEM

The great John Curtice [professor of politics at the University of Strathclyde] tells *Today* that Shropshire North represents a political earthquake – if the Richter Scale goes up to 10, this is 8.5. All this in a constituency that voted 60% Leave in 2016 ...

Will 4:15 a.m. on 17 December 2021 – the moment the result was declared – mark the opening whistle on the endgame for the Johnson premiership? If it is shown that he has lied to Parliament over the flat and the parties in the next few weeks, it could well have done so, and 'Oswestry' will forever be the moment when England *profonde* turned on him. But, if he does go, I fear it will not be with dignity or decency.

During the last few weeks, it's been hard to distil the political frenzy. It still is and, given Shropshire North, it will be for quite a time. Meanwhile, Omicron, which can neither find Oswestry on the map or *Today* on the dial, marches relentlessly on.

Omicron turned December 2021 into a month of near relentless anxiety. Chris Whitty caught this well at a Downing Street press conference on Wednesday the 16th when he said 'records will be broken a lot in the next few weeks ... We have two epidemics one on top of the other', on the day when Lady (Heather) Hallett, the former vice-president of the criminal division of the Court of Appeal, was named as the head of the Covid inquiry.

The other inquiry into the alleged 'parties' suffered another spasm on 17 December Simon Case had to recuse himself from it when it emerged that exactly a year earlier his private office had held a one-hour quiz. Simon had not played himself but had walked through into his own office while it was underway. The formidable Sue Gray replaced him – a lady who takes no prisoners, who did standards and ethics in the Cabinet Office for years and is now a second permanent secretary in Michael Gove's Levelling Up, Housing and Communities Department handling constitutional affairs. Still more parties came her inquisitional way:

MONDAY 20 DECEMBER 2021

This morning's *Guardian* runs a photo taken in May 2021 of a 'party' in the No. 10 back garden following a press conference. Johnson says: 'Those were meetings of people at work talking about work.' Starmer says: 'Just look at the photo.' Will this ever end?

Not for a good while.

One element of consistency marked the month, however. Johnson and his Cabinet resisted re-imposing a lockdown in England despite the surge in new cases. On Christmas Eve, the Office for National Statistics (ONS) released figures showing that in the previous week 1 in 35 had Covid in the UK (2.7 per cent of the population). What enabled the government to hold this line was what Dr Jenny Harries of the Health Security Agency called 'a Christmas glimmer of hope' provided by studies indicating that Omicron was a swift transmitter but less of a hospitaliser than Delta.

The Queen – as ever head of state *and* exemplary citizen – had cancelled Christmas at Sandringham with its sizeable family gathering for a slimmed-down occasion at Windsor, from where she broadcast her Christmas message to country and Commonwealth. Wearing the brooches she wore on her honeymoon in 1947, with Prince Philip's photo beside her, she said that 'one familiar laugh' would be 'missing this year' and talked of his gift for squeezing fun out of any circumstance. Looking forward to her Platinum Jubilee year, she hoped it would provide 'a chance for everyone to have a sense of togetherness.'[65] Place all her speeches together since the spring of 2020 and you have a sense of what an extraordinarily apt and effective Queen of the pandemic she was.

The following day I attempted 'SOME BOXING DAY THOUGHTS THROUGH AN ORKNEY WINDOW':

Slightly grey and a bit blowy compared to yesterday's bright, cold, jewel of a day.

What can be said about 2022 with any degree of certainty? That it will be both politically and epidemiologically significant; a benchmark year, but in which way and to what degree none of us can say. We *can* be sure that there will be other crises, dislocations and causes for anxiety or sadness (Heaven forbid we should lose the Queen).

Will Johnson last the coming year? Has his premiership been damaged beyond repair? Can he – or would he – totter on brazenly regardless? … The latest blast comes from Max Hastings, his old editor on the *Daily Telegraph*, in a column in *The Times* on Christmas Eve. Max argues (and I agree with him) that: 'we should not hanker for giants to lead us, whether in business, government or institutions. We should seek instead competent, reasonably honest men or women who are unafraid of hard work and responsibility.'[66]

I long for the day when the flow of ink (including mine) slows to a trickle about that man. He has become a national obsession to a deeply unhealthy degree. 'People live by narrative', he told [a] … journalist in August,[67] in yet another example of the hubris (to think that *he* could be the creator and shaper of some kind of master narrative for our times is delusory, even ludicrous) … Living in the Johnson premiership is like having a stone in your shoe every day.

I longed in vain, as we shall quickly see.

But, putting the prime minister's character on one side, 'yet more waves of pandemic; wars; climate dislocations and events; the Union question – that will be the big stuff'. I put my pen down and gazed out of the window over Scapa Flow in pursuit of solace. It worked – for a while.

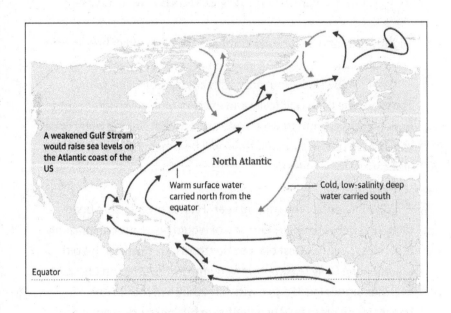

A weakened Gulf Stream would raise sea levels on the Atlantic coast of the US

North Atlantic

Warm surface water carried north from the equator

Cold, low-salinity deep water carried south

Equator

2

Who Belongs to Glasgow?

It's very irritating when they [world leaders] talk, but they don't do.

Queen Elizabeth II, overheard at the Welsh Senedd, 14 October 2021

Look again at that dot. That's here. That's home. That's us. On
it everyone you love, everyone you know, everyone you ever
heard of, every human being who ever was, lived out their lives.
The aggregate of our joy and suffering, thousands of confident
religions, ideologies, and economic doctrines, every hunter and
forager, every hero and coward, every creator and destroyer of
civilisation, every king and peasant, every young couple in love,
every mother and father, hopeful child, inventor and explorer,
every teacher of morals, every corrupt politician, every 'superstar',
every 'supreme leader', every saint and sinner in the history of our
species lived there – on a mote of dust suspended in a sunbeam.

The astronomer Carl Sagan musing on Earth as viewed from space
in *Pale Blue Dot: A Vision of the Human Future in Space*, 1994

Glasgow is none too strong on sunbeams in November. But Clyde-
side was fleetingly and crucially at the epicentre of our 'mote of dust'
between 31 October and 13 November 2021. It was a fitting place
for world leaders to contemplate the fate of the 'pale blue dot', as
it was through the west of Scotland that the world's first sustained
industrial take-off roared and raced in the eighteenth and nine-
teenth centuries along a riverside that belched coal smoke, hissed
with steam, and rattled with the sound of metal-bashing until the
riveting finally stopped in the last decades of the twentieth century,

when the 'Asian Tigers' (Hong Kong, Singapore, South Korea, and Taiwan) took away most of its shipbuilding business.

The earliest phase of what Earth scientists now call the Anthropocene[1] spoke with a Scottish accent. This was the central belt of Scotland into which Adam Smith, the begetter of modern political economy, was born in 1723. As his biographer, Jesse Norman, wrote shortly before himself becoming a Treasury minister in Whitehall: 'For a mother like Margaret Smith, ambitious for her clever younger son, Glasgow was a glimpse of the future.'[2]

Smith earned 'his place among the immortals', wrote Norman in 2018, by setting himself 'to address the foundational question of how far the pursuit of individual self-interest through cultural and market exchange can yield economic growth and socially beneficial outcomes.'[3]

The stark question facing the political guardians of 'the pale blue dot' gathered in the shade of Titan, the huge crane symbolising Scotland's global engineering and maritime economic apogee, was: could they, between them, do an Adam Smith for our times while combatting and mitigating the harmful man-made physics and chemistry that have been at work every second since the Earth's crust, its seas, its oceans, its atmosphere, began to be exploited by the dominant species at what would later become unsustainable levels? With 197 nations involved, several of whom were furiously raging together (to borrow from Handel's *Messiah*), it was going to be the loftiest of tall orders.

The fact that it was our prime minister in the chair was but one of the plentiful reasons for pessimism. His gifts, as they say in HR, very definitely lay in other directions. For example, in his finest 'Bertie Booster' mode,[4] he declared on 19 October, the day his government unveiled its Net Zero Strategy ahead of the Glasgow meeting,[5] that Britain could meet its target 'without so much as a hairshirt in sight'[6] – a forecast that did not exactly foster confidence among the higher ranks of scientists and analysts.

Somehow, crucial steps needed to be taken collectively to answer the 'foundational question' of our day. Some had been taken already in the weeks running up to the Glasgow summit, and two big ones in the course of a single day: 21 September 2021. President Xi Jinping announced that China would cease funding the building of coal-fired power stations abroad (but not at home in China). And Joe Biden said the United States would double its climate change budget to $11 billion by 2024 to help poorer countries deal with existing consequences of global warming and mitigate future changes.

Thus began a see-saw pattern of cheering and depressing developments in the run-up to the Glasgow conference. Its host was in Washington the day Biden made his announcement. I noted in my diary for 22 September:

> Johnson returns to New York to address the UN. He rightly says COP26 will be 'a turning point'; then, in a passage of breathtaking unawareness, says humanity has to 'grow up' about climate change ('The adolescence of humanity … must come to an end … It's time for humanity to grow up') – this from the man whose life-long project has been to prolong adolescence beyond all previous known limits, to pinch a line from my great hero, Tom Lehrer.

Maybe this more sober and serious prime minister would be a very different figure from the 'music hall' version – ego-heavy and detail-light – that had so often been evident on the Whitehall and Westminster stage hitherto.

These were among the 'THOUGHTS ON THE EVE OF COP26' that I placed in my diary on 30 October 2021. 'It is', I ventured, 'seriously cursed by a quartet of factors':

> 1: Its complexity (what to do? How to do it? By when? How to measure it?)
> 2: Herding 197 countries into some kind of (a) general agreement and (b) hard pledges and plans for their contributions to meeting the goals agreed at Paris in 2015.

3: The problems posed by three countries in particular (China, India, Russia – with Saudi Arabia, Turkey and Australia bringing up the tail). 4: Combatting a sense of fatalism that it's all too difficult and probably already too late.

But the coming decade *is* the last chance the world has for keeping temperature to no more than 1.5°C higher than pre-industrial levels (the current trajectory is a ruinous 2.7°C). The *New Scientist* this weekend reports that Alok Sharma's and the UK delegation's primary purpose is 'keeping 1.5°C alive').[7]

For me, as COP26 began, the $100 billion that the richer nations were to donate to the poorest ones was

of talismanic importance. In essence, it is to be the compensation paid by those countries that did best by scraping the 'frozen energy' out of the world's coal seams and converting it into the world-transforming industries that took hold after '1750 when human activities started disrupting Earth's natural equilibrium'.[8] It was this plundering of the earth's fossil bounty, plus the scientific dividend of the Enlightenment, that gave these countries 2 ½ centuries of economic growth the like of which the earth had not seen before.

The invoice for it has finally come in and Glasgow will be crucial in determining whether or not it will be paid in full and on time. Never in world history has such a debt been run up in so short a time.

Here the Adam Smith connection becomes critical:

One of the most crucial factors in reaching 1.5°C will be the harnessing to the cause of that very full-on capitalism which set the pace post-1750. Mark Carney, former Governor of the Bank of England and now the UN's Special Envoy on Climate Action and Finance, is the Adam Smith-of-our-day on this.

His argument is summarised in a piece in today's *FT Weekend*:
'We cannot get to net zero [carbon emissions by 2050] by flipping
a green switch. We need to rewrite our entire economies.' The
so-called COP Finance Strategy argues that the entire financial
system must be 'entirely focussed on net zero'. He concludes that
'Hard numbers in service of all people and our planet – that's the
real bottom line.'[9]

'From now on', I concluded, 'creating the wealth of nations has to
become inseparable from the survival of nations. Fossil fuels made
the modern world possible. They could also be its dismantler.'

On the eve of COP26, Boris Johnson was in Rome for a meeting
of the G20. Against the striking background of the Colosseum, it
was as if he had absorbed a rise-and-fall-of-civilisations theme and
an attack of the Arnold Toynbees* (to which Harold Macmillan
had sometimes been prone)[10] from its sun-touched ruins when he
held forth to the television news cameras. To Sky's Beth Rigby, he
said of Glasgow: 'The whole of humanity will be in the ring ... The
foes of humanity are political apathy and indifference ... I think it's
going to be very difficult.'[11] For the BBC's Laura Kuenssberg, he
summoned an image of the barbarians at the gate: 'Either COP succeeds or it's the Dark Ages.'[12]

Over the next two weeks, my diary recorded the swivelling
moods of COP26 as 30,000 people descended upon Glasgow –
negotiators, leaders, evangelists, demonstrators, and cynics alike;
every ripple of activity captured by a media caravanserai of heroic
proportions. It was as if a small town had landed inside Glasgow's
city limits. The spectrum of humanity was vast, stretching from
the elfin secular-saint Greta Thunberg to the grimly granitic Sergei
Lavrov, Russian foreign minister ('Why is 2050 not negotiable?').
As for the G20, it underachieved. It called for 'meaningful and

---

* Toynbee was, for a time, a hugely influential world historian who chronicled the fate of
civilisations with verve and width.

effective action' and re-committed to 1.5°C but, crucially, it gave no date for ending the use of fossil fuels.

The events of COP26 panned out as follows:

MONDAY 1 NOVEMBER 2021 (DAY 1)

On the first full day of COP26, the UK deploys its two greatest instruments of soft power – the Queen and her friend Sir David Attenborough. The pair of ninety-five-year-olds mobilise history and their sense of its grand sweeps in their pitches to the world. Speaking by video-link from Windsor, to which she is confined on doctors' orders, the monarch declares:

> It has sometimes been observed that what leaders do for their people today is government and politics. But what they do for the people of tomorrow – that is statesmanship.
>
> I, for one, hope that this conference will be one of those rare occasions where everyone will have the chance to rise above the politics of the moment, and achieve true statesmanship.
>
> It is the hope of many that the legacy of this summit – written in history books yet to be printed – will describe you as the leaders who did not pass up the opportunity; and that you answered the call of those future generations ... History has shown that when nations come together in common cause, there is always room for hope.[13]

David Attenborough, who is in the conference hall in person, shows himself, yet again, to be the great lyricist of the natural world who, seemingly effortlessly, can twin scientific evidence with beauty and truth:

> Everything we have achieved in the last 10,000 years has been enabled because of the [climate] stability during this time. The global temperature has not wavered over this period by more than either plus or minus one degree Celsius – until now ... Is this how

our story is due to end? A tale of the smartest species doomed by that all too human characteristic of failing to see the bigger picture in pursuit of short-term goals ... We have to rewrite our story.[14]

The pulse of history seems to fly across the room, even managing to arouse a sleeping Joe Biden, who said: 'We meet with the eyes of history upon us.'[15]

'History' is in for a swift disappointment. India, one of the top three polluters, at last produces its target, and it casts a pall across Glasgow: net zero by 2070 (i.e. twenty years too late), though it pledged to cut its emissions in half by 2030.

TUESDAY 2 NOVEMBER 2021 (DAY 2)

A pattern formed of good news tinged with bad. Over 100 countries sign a pledge for a 20 per cent reduction in methane emissions by 2030 but China, Russia, and India declined to do so. Another pledge – to end and reverse deforestation by 2030 – is made by 122 nations including Brazil.

The BBC's *Panorama* programme reports an analysis produced by the Meteorological Office showing that unless the world takes significant action on emissions, Europe can expect a so-called Lucifer-style heatwave (i.e. above 48°C) every year by 2100.

WEDNESDAY 3 NOVEMBER 2021 (DAY 3)

Finance day. Crucial. Speaking on the *Today* programme the previous day, Mark Carney has said this will determine whether or not there would be capital for 'financing the way things need to go'. Would global capitalism bend its arc to serve the overriding need? Carney managed to mobilise 450 of the world's leading financial institutions which, between them, undertake that 40 per cent of global finance will be devoted to climate-change purposes. Frans Timmermans, the ever-fluent vice-president of the EU Commission and its climate chief, tells Channel 4 News that the world will be 'sanctioned by nature if we don't act'.

The daily downer? Over forty countries agree to phase out coal-burning power stations – but not China, the US, India, or Australia.

THURSDAY 4 NOVEMBER 2021 (DAY 4)
There is concern that a loophole in the coal deal will enable countries to continue burning it until 2050.[16]

FRIDAY 5 NOVEMBER 2021 (DAY 5)
A climate pilgrimage comes to town. Addressing a packed Glasgow Square filled with parents, children, and young people, the voice of 2050 (and beyond), Greta Thunberg, describes COP26 as 'a two-week long celebration of business-as-usual and blah, blah, blah' – which is pretty well what Queen Elizabeth II has been overheard saying in the foyer of the Welsh Senedd the previous week. John Kerry, the US climate envoy, says he doesn't blame Greta for her frustration: 'We are behind where we ought to be.'

Where were they after week one? On the BBC *News at Ten*, its science editor, David Shukman, cites an International Energy Agency report which calculates that, so far, the agreements (on methane, forests, and coal) add up to a 1.8°C temperature rise. In the next week, COP26 would have to lift itself to a new level. However, to adapt Immanuel Kant's great line about humanity, out of the crooked timber of negotiation, nothing straight was ever made.

SATURDAY 6 NOVEMBER 2021
There are worldwide climate protests. Tens of thousands pack the streets of Glasgow.

MONDAY 8 NOVEMBER (DAY 6)
Barack Obama, who has lost none of his mastery over words or his sense of timing in their delivery, tells the delegates: 'We cannot afford hopelessness.' The conference concentrates on countries most at risk from rising sea levels.

TUESDAY 9 NOVEMBER (DAY 7)

Gloom falls upon me and my diary: 'There is more than a whiff of pessimism blowing around Glasgow. Climate Action Tracker says we are still on course for 2.4°C with what has been agreed so far. That is *disastrous*.'

The Climate Action Tracker examines countries' pledges for the next decade. It finds that carbon emissions will be twice as high in 2030 as they would need to be if the world is to stay below 1.5°C.[17]

Suddenly the gloom lifts. It's announced unexpectedly that the US and China have agreed to put aside their multiple differences and work together on climate for the next decade. In what looks like a long-in-the-making piece of bilateral diplomacy, the two super-powers pledge to take 'enhanced' action in three particular ways:

1: Cutting carbon emissions
2: Enforcing bans on illegal deforestation
3: Agreeing to 'phase down coal consumption' from 2026 and 'make best efforts to accelerate this work'

John Kerry says that on climate change, 'co-operation is the only way ... This is not a discretionary thing, frankly, this is science, it's maths and physics that dictate the road we have to travel.'[18] Kerry compares it to negotiating nuclear arms agreements in the Cold War: 'You have to look beyond the differences sometimes to find a way forward.' The Chinese lead negotiator, Xie Zhenhua, says: 'We hope this joint declaration will help to achieve success at COP26.'[19]

The big, immediate question – as Xie indicated – is whether this surprise deal will set the Clyde alight for the last two days of the conference.

The UK government's chief scientist, Sir Patrick Vallance, adds to this a sense of longer-term possibility. After delivering a lecture, he compares the Covid and climate crises in a BBC interview. Climate is a far bigger problem than Covid, which might be a two-to-three-year event rather than a fifty-to-one-hundred-year problem (by this,

I assume he means if we tackle climate successfully; if we don't, it's a forever problem). 'In the pandemic it took a concerted, worldwide effort to come up with vaccines, drug treatment [and] understanding what behavioural change is necessary – the same is true for climate.' And here comes the optimism:

> The technologies we need are either here or are in development. If we implemented them now and scaled up, a lot of change then takes place in terms of climate emissions.
> The second reason for hope is we've got a whole generation that's absolutely determined to do that. So there's behaviour change already happening right across the globe.[20]

Johnson returns to Glasgow declaring that 'there is still a huge amount to do', as the conference officials produce a seven-page draft communiqué.

THURSDAY 11 NOVEMBER 2021 (DAY 10)
No breakthroughs yet on finance or fossil fuels. There is a rising expectation that the conference will run on into the weekend. Reports suggest that the draft communiqué talks of 'phasing out fossil-fuel subsidies', but it is feared that the Saudis will resist that.

FRIDAY 12 NOVEMBER 2021 (DAY 11)
COP26 overruns. The draft communiqué does not keep 1.5°C alive. The sticking points remain finance and fossil fuels.

SATURDAY 13 NOVEMBER 2021 (TWELFTH – AND FINAL – DAY)
Alok Sharma opens the proceedings by declaring: 'This is the moment of truth for our planet.' Frans Timmermans says: 'Don't kill this moment.' News seeps out that India is pushing back on fossil fuels. Adam Vaughan documents the next developments for *New Scientist*:

> 6:20 [a.m.] Reuters breaks the news that India, China, the USA

and the EU are meeting on coal. They are filmed haggling in a huddle on the conference floor.

9:00 [a.m.] The communiqué emerges. Its key words on coal have been watered down from coal to be 'phased out' to 'phased down'. [It emerges later that the change in wording was the work of the Indian environment minister, Bhupender Yadav.][21]

A tearful Alok Sharma says: 'I apologise for the way this unfolded.' He was later reported as saying that China and India were going to have to 'explain themselves to the most climate-vulnerable countries in the world.'[22] The UN secretary-general, António Guterres, says: 'The world is still knocking on the door of climate catastrophe.' Sharma claims, 'we're going to need a few years to judge' the outcome of COP26.

True – but those haunting figures remain:

1.1°C: Now
1.8°C: If all the Glasgow pledges are fulfilled
2.4°C: Still likely

I wrote in my diary later that evening: 'For all the agreement that the nations would return to COP27 in Cairo* next year with stronger pledges, there was no disguising it. An air of underachievement – of opportunity lost – hung over the Clyde like a pall of carboniferous fog.'

As the naturalist Chris Packham pithily put it the evening before that dispiriting last day in Glasgow: 'We need to lock up that carbon and rebuild that diversity.'[23] At the time of my writing this chapter (Christmas week, 2021), we still do – and most likely will do for a perilously long time. We all belonged to Glasgow in November 2021, and COP26 let us down. The consequences of the Anthropocene scarcely loosened their grip.

* It was, in fact, in the city of Sharm El-Sheikh.

3

Mr Johnson Helps the Police with Their Inquiries

On Mr Johnson's watch, during the most severe pandemic
in more than a century and on the eve of the burial of the
monarch's consort, Number 10 was turned into a nightclub.

Andrew Rawnsley, *The Observer*, 16 January 2022[1]

DAVID DAVIS: Like many on these benches, I have spent
weeks and months defending the prime minister against often
angry constituents. I have reminded them of his successes in
delivering Brexit and the vaccines, and many other things.
But I expect my leaders to shoulder the responsibility for
the actions they take. Yesterday the prime minister did the
opposite of that, so I will remind him of a quotation that
will be altogether too familiar to him. Leo Amery said to
Neville Chamberlain: 'You have sat too long here for any
good you have been doing ... In the name of God, go.'

THE PRIME MINISTER: I must say to my right hon.
friend that I do not know what he is talking about. I
do not know what quotation he is alluding to.

Prime Minister's Questions, 19 January 2022

At Number 10, the prime minister and officials broke
lockdown laws. Brazen excuses were dreamed up. Day
after day, the public was asked to believe the unbelievable.
Ministers were sent out to defend the indefensible –
making themselves look either gullible or foolish ...

> Trust matters. It matters to our Parliament. It matters for
> the long-term protection and well-being of democracy.

Sir John Major, lecture to the Institute for Government, 9 February 2022

How could I have hoped on Boxing Day 2021 that the new year would see the cataract of ink spilt daily – even hourly – on the prime minister somehow abate for a time at least? The wrathful gods of politics enjoy their work too much to pay short visits – especially when their target is as irresistibly inviting as Boris Johnson, floodlit in hubris and dazzling in his shamelessness – a shamelessness that shamed his country and its political system.

My wishful thinking in those Boxing Day thoughts from an Orkney window went the way of so many of my political forecasts over the years. Far from fading, the matter of the prime minister's character evermore became the theme that ran like a corrosive seam through our national, public, and political life for the remaining eight months plus five days of the Johnson premiership. The distorting effect of this was that almost everything came to be refracted through the prism of 'the Boris question'.

It had its peaks and troughs, of course. At a particularly low moment, a veteran Conservative, whom I greatly admire, cried out during one of our conversations: 'He defiles everything he touches.'[2]

Future historians may mock such sentiments that portray Johnson as if he were all four horsemen of the apocalypse rolled into one. But that is how it felt on the bleakest days and weeks. It was a misuse of the highest office in the land beyond all previous imaginings. It was, as I suggested to Henry Mance in an interview for the *Financial Times*, 'a bonfire of the decencies'.[3]

In the first days of January 2022, the pacemaker for the 'character question' was the refurbishment of the Downing Street flat. Christopher Geidt was once again on the prime minister's case. What a contrast they made – the tall, kempt, ever-discreet ex-solider, diplomat, and courtier, the sheep farmer from across the Minch in the Isle of Lewis summoned to do the state very considerable service. The very incarnation of the 'good chap' tradition of public service, a man for all seasons, reliable to his last fibre (and, in private, possessing a very nice line in self-irony), speaking truth unto the ever unkempt, indiscreet, ill-disciplined, self-serving figure who, to his every last fibre, was a disrupter of all the traditions and decencies of public life. Geidt vs Johnson was – and will remain – the stuff of drama in which television delights. The series, when it is made, will have everything: power, money, deception (wilful or unintended), and a whiff of royalty (given Geidt's time in the service of the Queen) – *The Courtier and the Cad*. The Americans will love it. So will we.

In real life, the story erupted like a spurt of volcanic lava on 6 January 2022, the feast day of the Epiphany, in the form of those exchanges between Geidt and Johnson about the refurbishment of the Downing Street flat that took place in December 2021 but which had not until that day been made public. At issue was the failure to provide Geidt with what became known as the 'missing exchange' between Johnson and Lord Brownlow who, as we have seen, had initially come up with the money for the flat's redecoration. In a letter dated 21 December 2021, the prime minister offered Lord Geidt a 'humble and sincere apology' for not giving him the WhatsApp exchanges between himself and Lord Brownlow, claiming that he had forgotten about them and had since changed phones.[4]

Four days earlier, Geidt had written Johnson a letter of cold fury:

> It is of grave concern to me that, neither at the time when the Cabinet Office was collecting information ahead of my report ... was any attempt made to check for information relevant to my inquiries, such as the Missing Exchange. I consider that the greatest possible care should have been taken to assemble all relevant material and this standard has not been met ... This episode demonstrated insufficient regard or respect for the role of Independent Adviser [on ministers' interests].[5]

I noted in my diary on 6 January that the 'test will come in the degree to which Johnson tightens the [independent adviser] system in the coming months. CG's letter to him of 23 December strikes me as putting Johnson on probation.'

In that letter of 23 December, Lord Geidt reprised his frustrations about the *Missing Exchange*, arguing:

[It exposed] a signal deficiency in the standards upon which the Independent Adviser and, by extension, the Prime Minister have an absolute right to rely in establishing the truth in such matters. Indeed, the episode shook my confidence precisely because potential and real failures of process occurred in more than one part of the apparatus of government. I am very grateful to have your apology for these shortcomings and to know of your determination to prevent such a situation from happening again.[6]

'If anything like it *does* happen', I noted in my diary on 6 January 2022, 'I'm sure Christopher will walk.' Walk he did – over a different issue – six months later.

It was as if a poltergeist had taken over Downing Street. The wretched thing now moved downstairs from the flat – seemingly bored with fixtures and fittings – into the Cabinet Room and garden, even into a wine chiller brought in by the private office to assist with Friday drinks. As if the creature did not have enough with which to play havoc, the Metropolitan Police got involved too, lest Covid laws and regulations had been broken amid the clinking of glasses, the rodent-like sound of nibbles being nibbled, and the rattle of suitcase wheels as replenishment stocks were brought in from a nearby 'offy'. No. 10 partied as people were dying alone, as families kept to the rules and stayed away from hospital wards and funerals. Downing Street succumbed to a seediness mired in insensitivity that continues to baffle me. These were intelligent and good people who carried with them a high sense of public duty. Some blew whistles their superiors either did not hear or declined to act upon.

The juxtaposition of carousing lawbreakers in Downing Street and Covid-induced suffering and bereavement on the part of those who stoically obeyed the restrictions bit deeply into national consciousness, and they will be lodged there as long as the Covid years and the Johnson premiership are recalled. 'Partygate', as the press inevitably (and lazily) shorthanded the scandal, quickly came to overshadow what (mercifully) the media did *not* call 'Geidtgate'.

On 10 January 2022, Paul Brand of ITN, utilising once more his well-placed source (or sources) close to the drinking circles of Downing Street, broke potentially the most damaging story of all. It took the form of a 'smoking email' circulated to a hundred Downing Street staff by Johnson's principal private secretary, the diplomat Martin Reynolds, on 20 May 2020, which invited recipients to a 'bring your own bottle' gathering that evening in the garden of No. 10 to make the most of the good weather. That very afternoon Johnson had taken the government's daily Covid press conference and re-emphasised the current regulations, which allowed for a meeting with *one* non-family member outside the home. Reports suggested that between thirty and forty people turned up at the Downing Street party and that they included Boris Johnson and Carrie Symonds. After ITN broke the story, Dominic Cummings, who was still in the prime minister's employ at the time (though he had gone home), tweeted that 'the trolley [i.e. Johnson] was there'. Another 'party' had now been swept up into Sue Gray's hoover bag.

Wednesday 12 January was one of those days at Westminster when Prime Minister's Questions turns into an electric storm. I wrote in my diary:

At Noon, a battered-looking Johnson opens with an apology followed by an admission that he *had* been at the gathering on 20 MAY 2020 for 25 minutes in the belief it was a work event not a party regarding, as he apparently does, the No.10 Garden as an extension of the office. Every party leader called on him to resign now. He countered each time with the need to wait for the results of Sue Gray's inquiry. He was grim-faced at the end.

The prime minister said something that struck me as self-delusory. He had, he said, come to make amends. How could he even if he resigned? The deed was done. The hurt caused. It could not be undone.

On the opposition benches, the sheer detestation of the man was in the air, as was total disbelief of his explanations and the sincerity of his words – with good reason, if later reports of what he said in the House of Commons Tea Room straight after PMQs are to be believed. 'We have taken a lot of hits in politics, and this is one of them,' he said, according to *The Times*. 'Sometimes we take credit for things we don't deserve and this time we're taking hits for something we don't deserve.'[7] This was not the line he had taken in the Chamber. Quite the reverse. If those reports are right, he did not mean a word of it.

This is what he said in public in the Commons:

I want to apologise. I know that millions of people across this country have made extraordinary sacrifices over the last 18 months. I know the anguish they have been through, unable to mourn their relatives and unable to live their lives as they want or to do the things they love. I know the rage they feel with me and with the government I lead when they think that in Downing Street itself the rules are not being properly followed by the people who make the rules. Though I cannot anticipate the conclusions of the current [Sue Gray] inquiry, I have learned enough to know that there were things that we simply did not get right, and I must take responsibility.[8]

At Prime Minister's Questions, Keir Starmer was acidly dismissive of the I-didn't-know-it-was-a-party line saying it was so ridiculous as to be offensive to the public, who thought he was 'lying through his teeth'. Starmer declared: 'The party is over, Prime Minister.'[9]

'But was it?' I asked in my diary on 12 January 2022:

KS claimed Johnson had broken the Ministerial Code without giving chapter and verse. It will need, I think, a clear-cut example of deliberately misleading Parliament to do it. That's the key. Will Sue Gray's report … cut such a key for the House of Commons to turn? Or will it be a case of the survival of the shameless. His 'apology' yesterday was, I'm sure, carefully constructed to reduce the chances, so far, of the code biting him fatally.

Two days later, another storm of breaking news *did* burst over Johnson's head, which, perilously for the prime minister, drew the Queen into the whole wretched business. I recorded:

FRIDAY 14 JANUARY 2022
Awoke to news of still more parties – 2 of them in No.10 the night before Prince Philip's funeral [16 April 2021] when the Queen sat in poignant isolation in St. George's, Windsor. They were both farewell parties which coalesced and spilled over into the fatal garden. Someone was despatched to the TESCO in The Strand with a suitcase to bring back more booze. There was drink. There was dancing. A scoop for the *Daily Telegraph*. A huge embarrassment.

James Slack, the outgoing No.10 Comms Secretary (whose farewell party it was), apologises unreservedly this morning. Late morning No.10 apologises to the Queen. Two more parties are added to Sue Gray's list. Two more nails in the Prime Minister's coffin?

Who knows?

But what can be said as I watch the light fall on a bright, cold day at the end of an extraordinary week? That Boris Johnson will go noisily. That when it comes, his departure will be low on grace, thin on dignity and heavily freighted with self-justification. It is likely to be epic. It is unlikely to be pretty. It could come swiftly. It could take quite a while. I could be wrong on all these counts. He may imitate Sydney Carton on the scaffold in *A Tale of Two Cities* ('It is a far, far better thing I do now than I have ever done before…').[10] But I doubt it.

On Friday afternoon, 14 January, Paddy O'Connell (BBC broadcaster, journalist, and friend) emailed setting up a chat which led me to have a go at how to 'unmake' a prime minister. I scribbled a few notes:

THE UNMAKING OF A PM

1: 'Walking' like a Test Match batsman of old. The Sydney Carton option … a thing of grace and dignity which will do his long-term reputation a great deal of good.

2: Sue Gray finding a clear and unarguable example of the PM knowingly misleading the H of C wd he act according to convention?*

3: 15% of his parliamentary party (54) put in 'no confidence' letters and a contest which he may or may not fight.

There is something deeply unseemly – grotesque, even – about the future of a premiership turning on a document produced by an admirable senior civil servant [Sue Gray] laying out who invited him to what and when and what for. Caked in a linguistic mess about what is 'a party', what is 'a gathering', and can 'a garden' be deemed to be 'an office'? What has become of us and our system of government and the good sense and the decencies on which it rests?

The following day (Saturday 15 January) I recorded most of those thoughts in a Zoom call with Paddy O'Connell for the 16 January

---

* The system assumes that the PM is *not* a 'wrong 'un'.

edition of BBC Radio 4's *Broadcasting House*. Meanwhile the electric storm crackled its way round Westminster, the newspapers, and the media outlets.

FRIDAY 14 JANUARY 2022
Andrew Bridgen, a longstanding backer of Johnson's, calls on him to resign.

Alistair Burt (ex-Minister; decent and excellent, as always) says on *Newsnight* that he does not think there is a route back for Johnson: 'These stories will haunt the government until there is a change … something seems to have gone badly wrong in the culture of No.10 … Politicians have to set the standard.'

Earlier on the ITN News at Six, Michael Gove acknowledged that these stories are terrible. But when asked if Johnson should resign, he replied: 'No, no, no, no.'

Rumours swirl of more revelations to come in the weekend papers. And, as if on cue, Saturday's *Daily Mirror* runs the story of a 'Friday drinks' habit in No. 10 illustrated by a picture of a wine chiller being delivered to Downing Street.[11] Seizing on the chiller, Starmer says, 'It's now in the national interest that he goes.' Two Conservative MPs add their voices (Tim Loughton, ex-children's minister, says Johnson's position is unsustainable; Tobias Ellwood, chairman of the Commons Defence Select Committee, says he should either leave or step aside).

The following day, Starmer, bolstered by a ten-point lead in an *Observer* Opinium poll (LAB 41; CONS 31), returns to the attack, talking of partying on 'an industrial scale' that 'broke the law' and about which the prime minister had lied – and that was a resigning matter. Breaking down the polling figures, *The Observer* suggests that 76 per cent think Johnson broke lockdown rules; 13 per cent thought he was telling the truth; 64 per cent do not; and 67 per cent believe the police should investigate what happened.[12]

The headline over Andrew Rawnsley's column in the same paper, in which he described the conversion of No. 10 into 'a nightclub', exclaimed that the scandal had reached a level 'that even the great trickster can't blag his way out of'.[13] But the 'blagging' had barely begun, for at its heart was Johnson's lifetime special subject – his own survival and self-promotion. It was, to adopt the words of his hero Winston Churchill in May 1940, as if his whole life had been but a preparation for this hour.

In fairness to Johnson, there were fleeting moments when genuine shame somehow broke through the carapace. One example occurred on Tuesday 18 January in an NHS facility, as it happened. Johnson had been out of sight for a few days, quarantined by an outbreak of Covid in his family:

18 JANUARY 2022…
Johnson surfaces … for a visit to the Finchley Memorial Hospital in North London where Sky's Beth Rigby pounces. Beneath his mask he looks ground down and worn out and he sounds it too. When BR touches on the Downing Street parties on the eve of Prince Philip's funeral, he hung his head and looked on the verge of tears. 'I deeply and bitterly regret that happened,' he said. 'I can only renew my apology to Her Majesty and to the country for the misjudgements that were made…' On the 20 May 2020 party-in-the-garden, he said 'I can categorically say nobody warned me. Nobody said it was against the rules.'

It feels like *the* day matters shifted decisively against the PM in his own party … As the gloriously forthright Beth Rigby told him in her hospital interview, people find his account 'ludicrous'.

The metabolic rate of British politics continued to soar. 'What a day,' said Sir Lindsay Hoyle after one of the most extraordinary Prime Minister's Questions of recent times. 'It was,' I wrote in my diary entry for Wednesday 19 January. 'Ahead of it, I reckoned Johnson was in a very stretching position. If his temperament broke through his contrition and he got partisan and angry it would look and sound terrible for him.'

There is a fascination that attaches itself to PMQs every Wednesday, when Parliament sits at twelve and ministers mobilise language for the purposes of combat and the arousal of enthusiasm on their own benches – the weekly 'High Noon' of British politics. It is the ultimate giveaway of character.*

The Johnson/Starmer combination had a special fascination because of the temperamental contrasts that came into play:

Cavalier	Roundhead
Intuitive	Forensic
Flippant	Earnest
Performance-obsessed	Evidence-driven
Insouciant	Careful
Entitled	Meritocratic

Their pre-politics formations and the professions they pursued reinforced these traits by the hour – Johnson a combat journalist whose columns dazzled with gaudy, attention-seeking look-at-me-ism rather than the fastidious pursuit of truth; Starmer, a human-rights lawyer who rose to become director of public prosecutions (DPP), careful in the use of evidence, precise, if a tad dull, in the use of language. A life devoted to the pursuit of stardom juxtaposed with a career of duty and public service. How many of these contrasts would PMQs highlight on Wednesday 19 January?

It began with a carefully stage-managed defection from Conservative to Labour by Christian Wakeford, MP for Bury South, who took his new place on the Labour benches to a mixture of howls and cheers. After welcoming his new recruit, Starmer turned to the theme of the day:

---

* *High Noon* being the classic 1950s Western, starring Gary Cooper as a brave lawman.

STARMER: Every week, the Prime Minister offers absurd and frankly unbelievable defences to the Downing Street parties, and each week it unravels. [Interruption].

MR SPEAKER: I have been elected to the Chair. I do not need to be told how to conduct the business. If somebody wants to do some direction, I will start directing them out of the Chamber.

STARMER; The Conservative Members are very noisy. I am sure the Chief Whip has told them to bring their own boos. [Laughter.]

MR SPEAKER: Order. Let us try to get on with questions. It is going to be a long day otherwise.

STARMER: First, the Prime Minister said there were no parties. Then the video landed [of Allegra Stratton], blowing that defence out of the water. Next, he said he was sickened and furious when he found out about the parties, until it turned out that he himself was at the Downing Street garden party. Then, last week, he said he did not realise he was at a party and – surprise, surprise – no one believed him. So this week he has a new defence. 'Nobody warned me that it was against the rules.' That is it – nobody told him! Since the Prime Minister wrote the rules, why on earth does he think his new defence is going to work for him?

The prime minister slips swiftly into his PMQ-trademark style in which he creates a mini weather system around himself – essentially a mixture of usually irrelevant abuse and a music-hall turn mixed in with a litany of his achievements. On some Wednesdays it's as if the letters 'QC' after Starmer's name are a personal affront to a prime minister not noted for his care with evidence or the depth of his preparation. This was one of those occasions:

JOHNSON: If we had listened to the right hon. and learned gentleman about Covid restrictions, which is the substance of his question, then we would have been in lockdown after July. This is the truth. If we had listened to the Labour Front Bench in the run-up to Christmas and new year, we would have stayed in restrictions, with huge damage to the economy. It is because of the judgements I have taken and we have taken in Downing Street that we now have the fastest-growing economy in the G7 and GDP is now back up above pre-pandemic levels. As for Bury South ... we will win again in Bury South at the next election under this Prime Minister.

The two party leaders continued to talk past each other:

STARMER: Not only did the Prime Minister write the rules, but some of his staff say they did warn him about attending the party on 20 May 2020. I have heard the Prime Minister's very carefully crafted response to that accusation; it almost sounds like a lawyer wrote it, so I will be equally careful with my question. When did the Prime Minister first become aware that any of his staff had concerns about the 20 May party?

JOHNSON ... He asks about my staff and what they were doing and what they have told me ... They have taken decisions throughout this pandemic – that he has opposed – to open up in July ... to mount the fastest vaccine roll-out in Europe and to double the speed of the booster roll-out, with the result that we have the most open economy in Europe, and we have more people in employment and more employees on the payroll now than there were before the pandemic began. That is what my staff have been working on in Downing Street, and I am proud of them.

After more along the same lines, Starmer unleashed the most fundamental question of all.

STARMER: If a Prime Minister misleads Parliament, should they resign?

JOHNSON: Let us be absolutely clear: the right hon. and learned Gentleman is continuing to ask a series of questions which he knows will be fully addressed by the [Sue Gray] inquiry. He is wasting this House's time. He is wasting the people's time.[14]

Not a view that either the House or 'the people' seemed to share. A few minutes later, the Chamber burst into dramatic life when David Davis, long-time Brexiteer and, in his own mercurial way, one of the grand old figures on the backbenches rose to his feet and delivered the words, taken from the Norway Debate, with which I opened this chapter.[15]

Johnson, Winston Churchill's biographer,[16] brazenly pretended he was a stranger to one of the most famous quotes [Leo Amery was citing Oliver Cromwell's dismissal of the Rump Parliament on 20 April 1653] in parliamentary history during a debate that was crucial to making Winston Churchill prime minister.

Johnson is without peer in the retail trade of political fibbing. At moments of trouble (for him) he will reach for the shelf laden with deceit and grab whatever comes to hand. In this activity, if no other, his political immortality is guaranteed. Wednesday 19 January 2022 witnessed a shameful PMQs in which the prime minister consistently declined to answer Starmer's key question about misleading Parliament. Depths were plumbed.

I noted in my diary on that date:

Iain Dale on *Newsnight* confirmed that David Davis did his 'Amery' at the request of some the younger Conservative MPs. The House fell silent at the moment the Speaker called DD as if sensing what was to come. He [Johnson] *did* resort to sneering – rolling his eyes and looking at his watch while Ian Blackford [SNP Leader at

Westminster] put his questions. And, at the end of his exchange with Starmer, he grew more and more enraged and overheated and gabbling.

Watching PMQs as it unfolded that day, I scribbled: 'His lack of real contrition showed when he began to grin and smirk and gesticulate mockingly at Blackford.'

The story would not lie down. Five days later, on Monday 24 January, ITN broke yet another 'smoking party'. And, for the first time, No. 10 admitted to it and to the PM's presence. They could hardly not as it was his own fifty-sixth birthday party, held in the Cabinet Room on the afternoon of 19 June 2020. It appeared that on his return from a school visit, his wife, Carrie, presented him with a birthday cake and the twenty-to-thirty people present sang 'Happy Birthday'. According to ITN, there was another party later that day in the Downing Street flat. No. 10 denied this last bit.

Paul Brand's story shot another jolt of electricity through the 'prime minister and the parties' story. Keir Starmer called Johnson 'a national distraction', adding 'he has to go'. Ian Blackford said that the prime minister 'has insulted everyone in the UK'. Robert Peston, commenting on his colleague's scoop on the ITN news, said it had been 'the worst day for a prime minister I can remember for a considerable time ... [his] defence now looks extremely shaky'.

Drama begat drama. The following day, Tuesday 25 January, I recorded:

A large pebble is dropped into the murky pond by the Met Commissioner, Cressida Dick ... when she tells the Police Committee of the Greater London Assembly that her Force is examining cases of possible criminality based on material passed to them by Sue Gray. Immediately there was speculation that this would delay publication of Sue's report until the police inquiry was completed ... No.10 put it out that the PM still believes he has not broken the law.

The most bizarre intervention came from Conor Burns, Northern Ireland minister and an arch-Johnson loyalist. Speaking of the prime minister's fifty-sixth birthday party in the Cabinet Room, he said: 'He was ambushed with a cake.' As for the victim of the cake, the prime minister told the House of Commons that he welcomed the police inquiry as it would 'give the public the clarity they need'.[17] I noted in my diary: 'The Met's involvement does take the whole affair up to another level. Reports suggest that the police are going to investigate 8 of the 17 cases Sue Gray examined.'

On Wednesday 26 January at PMQs, Starmer once more concentrated on what, from the beginning of the affair, I thought was the crucial terrain on which the Johnson premiership would founder – the requirements of the *Ministerial Code*.

> STARMER: The ministerial code says that: 'Ministers who knowingly mislead Parliament will be expected to offer their resignation'.
> Does the Prime Minister believe that applies to him?
>
> JOHNSON: Of course, but let me tell the House that I think the right hon. and learned Gentleman is inviting a question about an investigation on which, as you know, Mr Speaker, I cannot comment, and on which he, as a lawyer, will know that I cannot comment.

It wasn't clear if Johnson was referring to the police investigation or Sue Gray's. There followed an abbreviated history about vaccines, jobs – his standard displacement activity. The leader of the Opposition was not to be diverted.

> STARMER: I think the Prime Minister said yes, he agrees that the code does apply to him. Therefore, if he misled Parliament, he must resign.
> On 1 December, the Prime Minister told this House from the

Dispatch Box, in relation to parties during lockdown, that 'all guidance was followed completely in No.10.'[18]

He looks quizzical, but he said it. On 8 December, the Prime Minister told this House that 'I have been repeatedly assured since these allegations emerged that there was no party'.[19]

Since he acknowledges that the *Ministerial Code* applies to him, will he now resign?

JOHNSON: No.

Johnson followed this one-word reply to Starmer's key question with a diatribe against what he described as his opponent's 'opportunistic' behaviour throughout the Covid crisis[20] – Johnson's own, very personal version of political scat-singing.

The 26 January 'High Noon' reached a crescendo of mutual loathing:

STARMER: The reality is that we now have the shameful spectacle of a Prime Minister of the United Kingdom being subject to a police investigation, unable to lead the country and incapable of doing the right thing ... Is this not a Prime Minister and a Government who have shown nothing but contempt for the decency, honesty and respect that define this country?

JOHNSON: No, we love this country and we are doing everything in our power to help this country ... The problem with the Labour party today is that the right hon. and learned Gentleman is a lawyer, not a leader.[21]

On the subject of 'leaders', Theresa May, Johnson's predecessor, penned a letter to her constituents in Maidenhead on Friday 28 January: 'It is vital that those who set the rules abide by the rules ... Nobody is above the law.'[22]

As the voters of Maidenhead were absorbing the wisdom of their

MP, the law (in the form of the Metropolitan Police), I wrote in my diary on 28 January,

> drop another large pebble into the 'parties' pond. They have issued a statement saying they want the Gray Report to make 'minimal reference' to the events they are investigating lest it prejudices their lines of inquiry. Parliament wants the 'full Gray' and fast. The PM claims he does too. 'Gray light' would be highly unsatisfactory and, plainly, the instances the police are most worried about are the most serious. But how much delay would this cause? Just what are the parameters of a 'minimum reference' paragraph? How many individuals will the police need to talk to? Every one of them will need to be lawyered up. It could be months.

Looking back, the Johnson years in No. 10 will be infused with a perpetual breathlessness, too much to take in as events happened. As Johnson prepared to help the Met with their inquiries, *The Economist*'s 'Bagehot' columnist did us all a great service when he penned a paragraph of rich content and surpassing succinctness:

> Things are never dull around Boris Johnson. Since 2019 the prime minister has led the Conservatives to their biggest vote-share since 1979, shaken up politics, taken Britain out of the European Union, endured a pandemic, nearly died, had a child, struck a trade deal with the EU, got married, had another child and seen his net approval rating swing from +40 to -51 after revelations about potentially illegal parties in Downing Street. His repeated dishonesty – and a police investigation into the high jinks, launched on January 25th – make them the most damaging in a series of scandals. Others include scrounging £53,000 ... from donors to redecorate his residence and trying to prorogue Parliament illegally. If Napoleon was history on horseback, Mr Johnson is history on a pantomime horse.[23]

As the veteran journalist Andrew Neil, a former editor of *The Economist*'s Britain section, and still as penetrating as ever, put it that same weekend, 'This is no way to run an ancient, proud, and significant nation.'[24] Probably the finest line he has ever uttered on television.

Monday 31 January 2022 was a significant day in the rolling story of degradation in Downing Street. Sue Gray was to deliver what the Cabinet Office called an 'update' on her report to No. 10 late morning,[25] and Johnson would make a statement in the House of Commons at 3 p.m.

First, Dominic Cummings provided the warm-up in an interview with *New York Magazine*. The man has a great gift for choice remarks laced with acid asides:

> The fact that someone wins an election doesn't mean that they should just stay there for years, right? If you've got a duffer, if you think someone can't do the job, or is unfit for the job ...
>
> You know, as he said to me: 'I'm the fucking king around here and I'm going to do what I want.' That's not okay. He's not the king. He can't do what he wants. Once you realize someone is operating like that then your duty is to get rid of them, not to just prop them up.[26]

The piece is enlivened still more by the PM's obsession with his legacy. If true, it's pure 'Ozymandias, King of Kings' territory.* According to Cummings, Johnson wondered: 'What would a Roman Emperor do? So the only thing he was really interested in – genuinely excited about – was, like, looking at maps. Where could he order the building of things?' Cummings says Johnson fantasised about 'monuments to him in an Augustan fashion'.[27] I noted in my diary: 'The one permanent legacy/memorial we can be sure he'll leave is how *not* to conduct the British premiership.'

---

* After the famous poem by Percy Bysshe Shelley.

At 2:30 p.m., Sue Gray's twelve-page 'update' was published. It was one of those truly scarring days in British political history and I tried to capture as much when I reached for my diary:

> For all its redactions, it [Sue Gray's 'update'] was tough, telling, and terse – an indictment of a whole approach to government in terms of process, propriety, and, above all, people and strikingly sensitive to the hurt felt by the bereaved and the indignation of the rule-keepers. It showed up Johnson's behaviour for what it was – an affront to the decencies upon which our entire system of government rests. His place in the history of UK politics and government is now assured in that corner where the low and dishonest lurk in grim and perpetual infamy.
>
> The pages that follow [in the Gray update and Hansard] contain a great deal. But they come nowhere near to capturing the *shaming* of our country I felt this afternoon as I watched events unfold on television.
>
> Johnson's act of contrition was short. Almost instantly, he was back on his old twin-track of partisan abuse (including a serious smear of Starmer who was not involved in the Jimmy Savile case [as director of public prosecutions] plus an inflated litany of the government's achievements. Starmer made the finest speech of his career so far, carving up the PM's rhodomontade (the Conservative benches seemed to sense this – they were very quiet when Starmer outlined his case for the prosecution). Calling it 'a tissue of nonsense', as Johnson did, was a pathetic and still more demeaning response.

HIGHLIGHTS FROM SUE GRAY'S UPDATE

She offered 'general findings' based on the 'context' that 'Every citizen has been impacted by the pandemic. Everyone has made personal sacrifices, some of the most profound, having been unable to see loved ones in their last moments or care for vulnerable family and friends.'

These findings included the following judgements:

Against the backdrop of the pandemic, when the Government was asking citizens to accept far-reaching restrictions on their lives, some of the behaviour surrounding these gatherings is difficult to justify.

At least some of the gatherings in question represent a serious failure to observe not just the high standards expected of those working at the heart of Government but also of the standards expected of the entire British population at the time.

At times it seems there was too little thought given to what was happening across the country in considering the appropriateness of some of these gatherings, the risks they presented to public health and how they might appear to the public. There were failures of leadership and judgement by different parts of No 10 and the Cabinet Office at different times. Some of the events should not have been allowed to take place. Other events should not have been allowed to develop as they did.

The excessive consumption of alcohol is not appropriate in a professional workplace at any time ...

the [No. 10] garden was also used for gatherings without clear authorisation or oversight. This was not appropriate ...

Some staff wanted to raise concerns about behaviours they witnessed at work but at times felt unable to do so. No member of staff should feel unable to report or challenge poor conduct where they witness it. There should be easier ways for staff to raise such concerns informally, outside of the line management chain.

Sue Gray added the observation that the growth in size and range of the No. 10 staff in recent years had produced 'leadership structures [that] are fragmented and complicated' which 'has led to the blurring of lines of accountability' that 'should be addressed as a matter of priority'.

Her overall conclusion? That there was 'significant learning to be drawn from these events which must be addressed immediately across Government. This does not need to wait for the police investigations to be concluded.'[28]

HIGHLIGHTS FROM THE HOUSE OF COMMONS EXCHANGES
Boris Johnson responded to the report in a debate on Monday 31 January 2022.

> THE PRIME MINISTER: It is not enough to say sorry. This is a moment when we must look at ourselves in the mirror, and we must learn.

He would act 'by creating an Office of the Prime Minister, with a permanent secretary to lead No. 10'. He would be saying more about the steps they would take 'to strengthen Cabinet government, and to improve the vital connection between No. 10 and Parliament.'[29] To which Keir Starmer responded:

> Our national story about Covid is one of a people who stood up when they were tested, but that will forever be tainted by the behaviour of this Conservative Prime Minister. By routinely breaking the rules he set, the Prime Minister took us all for fools. He held people's sacrifice in contempt. He showed himself unfit for office ... he is a man without shame ...
>
> To govern this country is an honour, not a birthright. It is an act of service to the British people, not the keys to a court to parade to friends. It requires honesty, integrity, and moral authority ... Whatever people's politics, whatever party they vote for, honesty and decency matter.[30]

The aspirant prime minister landed several blows on the serving one, but it was a previous prime minister, in the slaying of whose premiership Johnson had played such a prominent part, who crafted the blade which flashed brightest amidst the exchanges on the Gray 'update'. 'Mrs Theresa May,' the Speaker said. The House tensed as she spoke:

> The covid regulations imposed significant restrictions on the freedom of members of the public. They had a right to expect their Prime Minister to have read the rules, to understand the meaning of the rules – and indeed, those around him to have done so, too – and to set an example in following those rules. What the Gray report does show is that No. 10 Downing Street was not observing the regulations they had imposed on members of the public, so either my right hon. Friend had not read the rules, or did not understand what they meant – and others around him – or they did not think the rules applied to No.10. Which was it?

'No, that is not what the Gray report says,' Johnson replied.[31] But it was. As we have seen, Sue Gray specifically said 'too little thought' had been applied by senior figures in Downing Street.

It had, I wrote later, been:

> A dreadful day. That one man should bring our politics and our public life to such a low ebb is unbearable. I know it will not last. I'm pretty sure that Johnson's successor will strive to show that he or she is 'anybody but Boris'. But today will be a low watermark in national life that will be long remembered.

The speaker, Sir Lindsay Hoyle, was appalled by Johnson's claim that, as director of public prosecutions, Starmer 'spent most of his time prosecuting journalists and failing to prosecute Jimmy Savile, as far as I can make out ...'[32]

The next morning, replying to a point of order, Sir Lindsay said: 'I am far from satisfied that the comments in question were appropriate on this occasion. I want to see more compassionate, reasonable politics in this House, and that sort of comment can only inflame opinions.'[33] Sir Lindsay generally carries a great-and-good force field around him, but even his chances of bringing about a favourable turn in Johnson's behaviour were remote during the grimly depressing early weeks of 2022. And the worst of his premiership, as it turned out, was yet to come.

The considerable bulk of the prime minister showed no sign of shifting, but other Downing Street figures began to walk. A trio of them left on 3 February: Martin Reynolds, the principal private secretary; Munira Mirza, head of the Downing Street Policy Unit (fiercely critical of Johnson's attempt to link Starmer with the Savile case);[34] and Dan Rosenfield, director of communications. Cummings, tweet-at-the-ready, pronounces that 'the bunker is collapsing'. The veteran and much-respected Conservative figure Malcolm Rifkind goes on *Newsnight* to declare, 'It's the beginning of the end.' Johnson's former ally, Andrew Bridgen, says: 'Cabinet ministers need to tell the prime minister the writing is on the wall.'[35]

If it were, would Johnson read it? If he did, he would disdain it. In a potentially significant signal of a growing rift between the prime minister and the chancellor of the exchequer, Rishi Sunak, referring to Johnson's claim about Starmer and Savile, declared: 'I wouldn't have said it.' (Sajid Javid would later say Keir Starmer 'deserves absolute respect' for the job he did as DPP.)

Sunak was announcing measures 'to take the sting out of a significant price shock', by which he meant the 34 per cent increase in energy costs that lay ahead (£9 billion extra from the Treasury to take £200 off everyone's energy bills plus another £150 for the poorest in society). The sense of a gathering economic storm was heightened on 3 February when the Bank of England raised interest rates by 0.5 per cent in the expectation that inflation would peak at 7.25 per cent in April. 'We are concerned that this inflation is going to get embedded,' said the governor of the Bank of England, Andrew Bailey.[36]

Johnson's shameful performance at the despatch box on the day of Sue Gray's 'update' illustrated the plight of the 'good chap' theory of government. *The Economist*'s 'Bagehot' caught its vulnerability in his column at the end of the week:

> In Parliament on January 31st, Sir Keir [Starmer] wound up with a simple attack on the prime minister. 'He is a man without shame.' Unfortunately, British politics relies on shame to function. The country still runs on the 'good chap' theory of government: the idea that politicians abide by the invisible lines of the constitution. An absence of legal constraints requires an abundance of personal restraint, and Mr Johnson has none. A bad chap can go a long way.[37]

In his *Guardian* column on 4 February, Martin Kettle expressed it pithily: 'Johnson owes his prime ministership to running against Britain's governing system.'[38]

How did the political market react to this extraordinary week? On Saturday 5 February, *The Times* published a YouGov poll:

> A third of those voting Conservative in 2019 think Johnson should resign.
>
> LABOUR 41; CONSERVATIVES 32; LIBERAL DEMOCRATS 10; GREENS 6.

The paper also reported that Johnson loyalists were muttering against Sunak, the more inflamed among them thinking the PM should sack his chancellor.[39]

A world away – in almost every sense – the Queen, at Sandringham to mark the seventieth anniversary of her father's death in the place where he died, renewed the pledge of lifelong service to her people that she made so compellingly on her twenty-first birthday in South Africa. As for her current prime minister, the political editors of *The Sunday Times*, Tim Shipman and Caroline Wheeler, report 'friends' of Johnson telling them: 'He's making very clear that they'll have to send a Panzer division to get him out of there.'[40] I note in my diary on 6 February:

> The frenzy continues unabated, and the story shifts to whether or not Graham Brady [chairman of the 1922 Committee of Conservative backbenchers] will receive letters getting the confidence question past the required 54 benchmark before Parliament goes into a 10-day recess on Thursday. One more big Johnsonian gaffe and my hunch is that the trigger point will be reached. Meanwhile, THE SHAMING OF BRITAIN continues. What a behavioural chasm separates our Head of State and our Head of Government.

In a newspaper column that same day, Sir Max Hastings declared: 'The experiment in celebrity government to which the Conservative Party committed us has failed, and is seen by the world to have failed. The foremost task for a successor is to restore Britain's reputation as a serious country.' Sir Max foresaw Johnson's life beyond No. 10 as

> skipping lightly across the landscape, amassing a fortune from his memoirs and from his stellar gifts as an entertainer. 'You see?' [he] will say, with that confiding, irrepressible, guilty-schoolboy grin which has borne him to a preposterous altitude of fame and power: 'It was all a jolly jape, wasn't it?' Not for the British people, Boris. Not for the British people.[41]

There were several moments in the unmaking of the Johnson premiership when it appeared that matters simply could not deteriorate further, only for them to promptly do so. This was one of them.

MONDAY 7 FEBRUARY 2022

A dreadful day in British political and public life. Keir Starmer was mobbed outside the MOD (he'd gone in for a briefing on Ukraine) by protestors, some of whom abused him as a friend of paedophiles and a 'traitor'. The police had to closely protect him and get him into a car.

Johnson described the behaviour as 'absolutely disgraceful' but continued to refuse to withdraw – or apologise for – his words in the H of C a week ago.

While watching the news, I scribble, 'It *is* truly dreadful. Another twist of the downward spiral of our politics.'

Almost exactly the words Dominic Grieve used on the ITN 10.

Julian Smith, David Lidington, and Tobias Ellwood urged Johnson to withdraw and apologise – but he wouldn't budge.

Chris Bryant was magnificent on CHANNEL 4 NEWS and laid the blame for those scenes squarely on Johnson's shoulders:

> 'It's deliberate. It's an attempt to incite a mob … it's profoundly dangerous … It's so un-British … This is despicable … The danger is that when politics is brought into disrepute … The prime minister could come to the House of Commons to apologise and properly withdraw those remarks … Everyone ends up dancing to his tune.'[42]

On the ITN 10, Bryant added: 'This is the mob ventriloquising Boris Johnson.'

The following day, as soon as he was able, Sir Lindsay Hoyle condemned from the speaker's chair those who mobbed Starmer and rebuked Johnson for what he said, declaring:

I know it has been reported that some [abuse was directed at Starmer] related to claims made by the Prime Minister in this Chamber, but regardless of yesterday's incident, I made it clear last week that, while the Prime Minister's words were not disorderly, they were inappropriate. As I said then, these sorts of comments only inflame opinions and generate disregard for the House, and it is not acceptable. Our words have consequences and we should always be mindful of that fact.[43]

No. 10 repeats that the prime minister will not apologise.

By this time, Downing Street had a new director of communication – Guto Harri (an ex-BBC journalist and a man with whom I had relished doing an occasional turn at the Hay Festival of Literature and Arts). He had served Johnson in his City Hall days and had now returned to help save his embattled friend. When he went to see Johnson the previous Friday to accept the job, the two saluted each other and launched into a joint rendition of Gloria Gaynor's 'I Will Survive'.

But would he? Just after 7 p.m. on the evening of Wednesday 9 February 2022, news broke that the Metropolitan Police's Operation Hillman would be sending more than fifty people in Downing Street and Whitehall a questionnaire on party gatherings, which they would have to complete and return within seven days. Mr and Mrs Johnson would be among them. The UK would rejoice in having a prime minister helping police with their inquiries. It might not be Gloria Gaynor time for long in No. 10.

I don't know if Sir John Major is familiar with Gaynor's oeuvre. I rather suspect not – though he certainly learned a few hard lessons on political survival in the 1990s. But on Thursday 10 February, the former Conservative PM played a very Major-ish soundtrack in the form of a lecture he delivered on the theme of democracy and trust in politics at the Institute for Government just across St James's Park, in the splendour of Carlton House Terrace. I thought it turned out to be *the* speech of his life. It broke through the crust of Johnsonism and mercilessly exposed its corrosive damage:

At No.10, the prime minister and officials broke lockdown laws.

Brazen excuses were dreamed up. *Day* after *day* the public was asked to believe the unbelievable. Ministers were sent out to defend the indefensible – making themselves look gullible or foolish. Collectively, this has made the government look distinctly shifty ...

And trust *matters* ... It matters to our Parliament. It matters to our country. It matters to our United Kingdom ... And it matters for the long-term protection and wellbeing of democracy.[44]

At the Q and A session after his lecture, Sir John was asked if a prime minister should resign if they had broken the law. 'That has always been the case,' he replied. He went on: 'The prime minister and our present government not only challenge the law, but also seem to believe that they – and they alone – need not obey the rules, traditions, and conventions – call them what you will – of public life.'[45]

John Major has, since leaving No. 10 in May 1997, rationed his interventions carefully. Here was a critical one which, in that last sentence, went to the heart of the matter – the bonfire of the decencies, the casting aside of the normal expectations of public and political life. His case was made all the stronger as John Major was the prime minister who first made *Questions of Procedure for Ministers*, as the *Ministerial Code* was then called, public in 1992 (previously it had been a Cabinet paper retained for thirty years).

Where did the Johnson Question stand in the second week of February 2022 after his Conservative predecessor-but-three had delivered his broadside from the lectern of the Institute for Government? Never in modern times had there been a prime minister whose departure had been so keenly anticipated by so many with such good reason.

Yet the political calculus was about to change not just for the UK but – in the *geo*political sense – for the world when the great accumulating friction ripping through the Russo–Ukrainian rim of eastern Europe was to explode along the riverbanks and through the wheat fields where so much wrecking-ball history had passed in the twentieth-century 'struggle for mastery in Europe', as A. J. P. Taylor described it.[46]

Even before the Russians attacked on three fronts at 5 a.m. on the morning of Thursday 24 February 2022, the Russo–Ukrainian War of 2022 had achieved a singular place in the history of conflict. A key element in our ability to follow the worsening sequence of events was the flow of Western intelligence assessments that were made available publicly in Washington and London almost as soon as they reached their customers in the White House and Whitehall. I don't know who invented this new kind of intelligence-led preventive diplomacy. It did not, in the end, deter the Russian military build-up from tipping into war, but it was very striking at the time.

For example, on 14 February, US Intelligence reported that Russia planned to invade Ukraine in two days' time. Sixty per cent of Russian land forces were massed on the border. We awoke on 16 February to find that Russia had *not* invaded overnight. The BBC cited the UK chief of defence intelligence as saying the Russians were bringing up more equipment and a field hospital. The following day the Ministry of Defence released a video which warned that 'an invasion could happen in the next few days'.

On Friday 18 February, I noted in my diary:

This is the day when it felt as if war really was coming. As Jens Stoltenberg [NATO Secretary General] said, Russia now had in place what it needs to be 'ready to invade without warning time'. They now have 190,000 troops around the periphery of Ukraine and all the equipment and back-up they require in the forward areas. Separatists move people out of the eastern provinces into Russia. Putin accuses Ukraine of human rights violations. Putin said 'those exercises are purely defensive in nature'. Nobody believes him ... The Beijing [Winter] Olympics ends on Sunday. In the small hours of Monday, Tuesday, or Wednesday the Russo–Ukraine war could begin.

As for the bigger impulse about to play out,

> I fear this is Putin's moment to place himself on the pantheon of –
> as he would see it – great Russian heroes. He's a destiny politician;
> a vanity politician with an excessive sense of personal destiny
> who sees *his* interests as coterminous with those of his nation.
> Many lives may be sacrificed to the dreadful conceit as Putin tries
> to bend the arc of history his way.

After a few more days of frantic preventive diplomacy, during which President Macron seemed briefly to be within reach of persuading Biden and Putin to meet at a joint summit, it happened.

> THURSDAY 24 FEBRUARY 2022
> I turn on Radio 4 at 6:30 a.m. to hear Lyse Ducette saying: 'The war
> has started'.
> As the light comes up over the Flow on a bright, cold wind-
> blown [Orkney] morning with a dusting of snow on Wideford Hill
> across the water. What a contrast it creates to the bleak, dark news
> from Ukraine.
> The Russo–Ukraine War 2022 has begun in earnest. It is
> impossible to see when and how it will end. Will it be a short, hot
> war contained on Ukraine territory surrounded by a serious and
> enduring Cold War 2, or, heaven forbid, will it spill over into NATO
> article five countries? I suspect the former, but I have no idea. It's a
> *huge* question – and geopolitics turns on it.

I'm a firm believer in the likelihood of first assessments going astray, but one of the purposes of keeping a diary is to remind oneself of this tendency, as well as being a replenisher of one's personal reservoir of humility.

> But here goes.
> This is my attempt amidst the shock and turmoil of the first hours.

SHORT-TERM, the easy bit first.

Oil, gas, and wheat prices soar. Gas up 45% today. Gazprom shares down by 34%. Russian stock market fell by 33%. FTSE lost £377bn worth of value.

MEDIUM-TERM. What is Putin's 'sinister vision' [as Joe Biden called it]?

The key questions are:

- Will he confine the roar of war to Ukraine, seek to contain it there and keep well short of tackling a NATO Article 5 nation? Could there be an unintended escalation (the mad tank officer scenario)? This would still be a very serious disruption of the former status quo. This would see a localised 'hot' war contained by a wider Cold War 2. But matters would move from *shock* to immensely *menacing convulsion* if he applies his 'model' to the Baltics, for example.
- Such a convulsion would raise direct confrontation between Russia and the United States and even the barely thinkable risk of a third world war. A third world war that would be different than world wars one and two in that, from the outset, everyone knows what the outcome would be if it went all the way – a nuclear exchange.

LONG-TERM. Let's assume contingency one happens i.e., localised hot war contained by a wider Cold War 2 which I reckon is the likeliest. Russia becomes seriously isolated economically and, therefore, ever more reliant on China as provider of financial succour and buyer of its critical raw materials, oil and gas, in a world economy where hydrocarbons are going to be of diminishing value in the long-term. Ukraine may come to be seen as the last throw of a fading former superpower. The danger here is that it could turn even nastier as it falls into a vortex of relative economic decline. For the world economy generally, this might stimulate an end to the long march towards ever greater globalisation for half a generation at least.*

If this contingency materialises, what consequences will it have for

1. US/China competition not just in economic terms but also for world influence?
2. The geopolitical postures of NATO and EU?
3. For the UK as a serious, upper-middle rank player in both the economic and the influence markets of the world? The Integrated Review is just under a year off the presses. It's already out of date and likely to become more so.

Putin has secured his place in history all right. He's reminded us of just what damage one man's vanity, inflamed by his demons and his delusions, can do in a matter of hours adding powerfully to the sense of vulnerability in the world.

Late February 2022 was one of those times when you could almost feel the dials of expectations being reset across the world as we waited to see how long Kyiv would hold out and the Zelensky government resist.

In the UK, Johnson's survival as prime minister remained a live question. On Sunday 27 February, the day Putin placed his nuclear forces on 'high alert', *The Sunday Times* ran a large poll of 4,500 people on the internal politics of Johnsonian Britain:

LABOUR 45%; CONSERVATIVES 32%; LIBERAL DEMOCRATS 11%

If those were the party shares in a general election next week, they would trigger a Conservative loss of 164 seats leaving a

---

* I owe this point to an old friend in British Intelligence, with much experience of China, Russia, and hydrocarbons, to whom I spoke on the telephone the morning I wrote this diary entry.

Parliamentary Conservative Party of 201. Labour would have 352 seats in the House of Commons. Half the Cabinet would lose their seats (including the prime minister). Only 9 per cent of those polled believed that Johnson 'tells the truth'.[47]

On Monday 28 February, President Biden uses his annual 'State of the Union' message to Congress to declare that 'the United States will defend every inch of NATO territory' and led a standing ovation for Ukraine.

The climate does not read the papers. On Tuesday 1 March, pretty well all of them carried the latest warnings from the UN's Inter-governmental Panel on Climate Change, in its regular summary for policymakers, that over 3 billion of the world's population could be vulnerable; that there is 'a brief and rapidly closing window' of opportunity to minimise the catastrophic consequences; that the percentage of the global population exposed to heat stress is pro-jected to rise from 30 per cent to between 48 and 76 per cent.[48] As I wrote in my diary on 1 March 2022, 'I fear that the war is taking all our minds off this. There is only so much attention/thinking power humans can apply to crises – and the immediate will always crowd out the rest (not that climate change isn't "immediate" – it is both immediate and relentless).'

At the end of the first week of the war, all the papers published terrible images of Babyn Yar, site of a memorial to 30,000 Jews shot by the Nazis when they took the city in 1941, being bombed by the Russians along with the television tower in close-by Kyiv.

The signs are that Putin's plan for a swift push on the Ukrain-ian capital are not going according to plan. The 40-mile column moving down from the north appears to have been held up by a combination of Ukrainian resistance, mechanical breakdowns, fuel-supply problems, and conscript Russian soldiers being unwill-ing to fight, plus vehicles getting stuck in the mud. One video flying around the world is of a Ukrainian tractor pulling a Russian tank away, chased by its shouting driver and the sound of someone else laughing intensely.

The other images are universally grim. The UN says the war has created 1.2 million refugees already, in the greatest crisis of its kind in Europe since the Second World War. In a superb column in *The Observer* on 6 March, Neal Ascherson (who has a special feel for the conflict-haunted lands of central and eastern Europe and the North European Plain), writes that:

> Here history is indeed trying to remember an old song: Moscow's obsessive wish to paralyse and subjugate the space between Russia and western Europe. A wish that didn't begin with Putin, or with Stalin's ring of satellites, but 300 years ago with Peter the Great and later, above all, with the Empress Catherine.

It was one of those newspaper columns you really wish had been read by its subject (maybe it was, but I suspect not; Putin's is one of those regimes whose courtiers tell the latest tsar what he wishes to hear rather than what he needs to know). One wonders how the probably ailing sixty-nine-year-old tyrant, in a hurry to secure his place in the Peter–Catherine–Stalin pantheon, might have reacted to this paragraph of Ascherson's:

> History doesn't repeat itself. It just tries to remember an old song it heard once. It may be that Putin's 24 February 2022 will turn out to be like Hitler's 22 June 1941 – the day he invaded Russia, doomed himself and Germany to destruction and made inevitable a divided Europe whose Cold War and barbed wire would last for half a century. But Putin isn't Hitler. He will die a disappointed old nuisance in exile somewhere, rather than by *Heldentod* suicide in his bunker. Both men qualify as psychopathic dictators, swaddled from reality in fantasies of geopolitical revenge. But Putin's grip on the Russian imagination is weaker than Hitler's on the Germans. And his use of police terror against his own people, though horrifying, is distinctly less effective.[49]

History itself felt overloaded. At the end of the second week of the war, a shrewd Walthamstow friend, Christine Dalton, caught this with vivid simplicity: 'It's like decades happening in a matter of days.'[50]

The conflict in Ukraine also aroused the prime minister's sense of history. Very swiftly, he pledged aid and support to the Ukrainians. The government sent 'Stinger' missiles, which the Ukrainians used to great effect against Russian tanks. There were reports of Ukrainian soldiers crying 'God save the queen' as they pulled the trigger.

On 11 March 2022, Day 16 of the war, I penned a 'reflection':

It's still immensely hard to absorb all that has happened since 24 February. Putin has punched a hole through Europe and torn apart any remaining 'never again' optimism that we might have had about war in Europe. The 'never again' feeling has simply gone. It *has* happened again – brutal war pursued by a tyrant thrusting into the heart of Europe on behalf of a country whose system of government and foreign policy are based on ingrained and shameless lying. There is peril in the air and pessimism stalks the land.

Perhaps the most remarkable encapsulation of the sense of peril is the talk of an endgame involving nuclear weapons. Let's eavesdrop on Joe Biden on 11 March addressing the House Democrats' retreat in Philadelphia:

The idea that we're going to send in offensive equipment and have planes and tanks and trains going in with American pilots and American crews – crews, just understand – and don't kid yourself, no matter what you all say – that's called 'World War Three'.[51]

'My fear', I wrote in my diary, 'is that unintended escalation could occur which takes on a life of its own beyond the control of either Russia or US/NATO.'

With a chilling historical resonance, diplomacy shifts to the Palace of Versailles with an EU summit chaired by President Macron issuing a 'Versailles Declaration' on 11 March. The twenty-seven member states collectively agree to rearm and to seek to become more autonomous on energy, food, and military equipment.

At a press conference afterwards, Macron contrasted Versailles 1919 with Versailles 2022. What he called the 'tragic turning point' of the Russian invasion of Ukraine had united Europe, whereas the Versailles conference at the end of the Great War had divided it: 'We want to be open to the world, but we want to choose our partners and not be dependent on anybody.'[52] This *could* have great significance for the path of globalisation and the unity of the EU itself. We, the UK, of course, were neither in the room nor at the table – which *is* highly symbolic of the margin to which Brexit and its aftermath are driving us. As the former head of the Diplomatic Service, Patrick Wright, once predicted in a conversation with me, Brexit would mean losing one of the boxing rings in which we once sought to punch heavier than our weight. As a people and polity, I don't think we're anywhere near appreciating the diminution of our status in the world – though we are absorbing fast the sounds of those ancient songs of which Neal Ascherson wrote.

SUNDAY 12 MARCH 2022

The Daltons come for tea. Andy Dalton very kindly brings me a copy of Edwin Muir's poems, his ONE FOOT IN EDEN collection. I'm very struck by a couple of lines from his 'Into Thirty Centuries Born':

'We meet ourselves at every turn In the long country of the past.'

It captures not only human nature at its worst and best but the remixed reprises therein, one of which we have been living in since 24 February – the terrible scenes of bombed hospitals and homes, the columns of refugees, the darkest forces in Europe seeking to subjugate a smaller neighbour. The big question is how extensive a mastery of Europe is Putin seeking?

The headlines have moved from Covid to the shores of the Black Sea, the banks of the Dnieper, and the road from Belarus to Kyiv, but the pandemic has not finished with us. There are now more patients than at any time for a year. The BA.2 version of Omicron is now the dominant one in the UK and it's more transmissible than the BA.1. ONS figures on 11 March show that 2.6 million have the disease (up from 2.4 million last week). One in eighteen have it in Scotland, one in twenty-five in England.

One of the inherent problems with the writing of really instant history is applying a sense of what episode or moment will remain of lasting significance once the ever-pacier juggernaut of journalistic attention has moved on and swerved a time or two. Blackpool, Saturday 18 March, was such an occasion, when the prime minister addressed the Conservative Party's Spring Conference.

He began vigorously and well. If Putin were to be victorious, it would be a 'green light to autocrats everywhere ... Putin has made a catastrophic mistake ... This is a turning point for the world'. Then, as I noted in my diary,

he insults 48% of the UK voting public, 650m people in the EU and 44m Ukrainians while revealing his inner self in its full ghastliness.

'And I know that it's the instinct of the people of this country, like the people of Ukraine, to choose freedom every time. I can give you a couple of famous recent examples – when the British people voted for Brexit, in such large, large numbers, I don't believe it was because they were remotely hostile to foreigners. It's because they wanted to be free to do things differently and for this country to be able to run itself.'[53]

This is DEEPLY objectionable on so many levels:

- The EU is not a tyranny. Ukraine wants to join it.
- Winning a free vote in an open society is in no way comparable to resisting a brutal and blood-stained invader.
- The 48% who voted Remain are not would-be aiders and abetters of tyranny.

That's about 850m people insulted in 4 sentences. No British premier has ever managed such a feat before. I suspect that Johnson's character is so deficient in terms of judgement and sensitivity that he cannot see what he has done to inspire such criticism. The terrible war in Ukraine had drawn attention away from his unfitness for office. Now it has contrived to place it centre stage once more.

It was a classic example of how to lose friends and not influence people. The reaction was fierce and immediate, as I recorded:

Guy Verhofstadt (former Belgium Prime Minister) described Johnson's comments as 'insane'.

Donald Tusk (former President of the EU Commission) says: 'Boris, your words offend Ukrainians, the British and common sense.'

Michael Heseltine says: 'Millions of Conservatives will be ashamed at so flagrant an attempt to exploit the horrors we see every day for party advantage.'[54]

I'd never heard my old friend, the Conservative peer Patrick Cormack, so upset as when we talked on the phone the following morning. I gave him my thoughts on the multitude of people the PM had insulted. Patrick felt a letter to *The Times* coming on – and I encouraged him warmly (it came the following Tuesday).[55]

In another conversation, another old friend, the Labour peer

Alan Howarth, advanced to me a new 'scrambled-egg theory' of the demise of a premiership – that as the pan heats up the beaten eggs are suddenly transformed into the scrambled product. I suggested, changing metaphors, that it could be a small 'last straw' that swiftly triggers the fall. Alan reckoned Johnson would be gone by the end of the year. So did I. The next day the Metropolitan Police began interviewing Downing Street party attendees, following up the 100-plus questionnaires they had distributed earlier.

Just over a week later, on Tuesday 29 March, the Metropolitan Police issued twenty fixed-penalty fines. No names were attached. The police said there could be more to come:

> PM's office say BJ and Simon [Case] *will* be named if they receive penalty notices. There is significance here. The police have found evidence that the law/guidelines were broken. Johnson had denied this (on 8 DEC) in the H of C. This shoves the story deeply and unequivocally into Ministerial Code country and, therefore, into a resignation matter (misleading Parliament).

The rolling story of the Downing Street parties gave an edge to Prime Minister's Questions as sharp as any I have known since I first became seriously interested in politics in the late fifties and early sixties. Wednesday 30 March 2022, which I subheaded 'THE MET, THE PM, AND THE LORD CHANCELLOR' in my diary, was a classic example:

> Johnson tries to hold his trench against incoming from the Met in the shape of those 20 (so far) penalty notices. His Justice Secretary and Lord Chancellor (who has, in that second role, sworn an oath to uphold the rule of law) Dominic Raab opened the day by acknowledging in a BBC TV interview that said notices showed there were 'clearly breaches of the regulations'.
> The PM (the keeper of the *Ministerial Code*) repeatedly refused to acknowledge this both at PMQs and during his appearance

before the H of C Liaison Committee later in the afternoon. He insisted he would not give 'a running commentary on that', telling the SNP's Peter Wishart at the Committee session: 'I'm going to camp pretty firmly on my position.'[56]

At PMQs, Starmer said: 'There was widespread criminality' and asked 'why is he still here?' after reminding Johnson of his denial on 8 DEC 2021, in the H of C, that he had denied that any guidance or laws had been broken.

But would this most brazen of prime minsters get away with it? After the squall at PMQs and inside the Liaison Committee on 30 March, I attempted my own political weather forecast:

The war has emboldened Johnson. The elastic has slackened. But it's still taut – and it's still there. The Downing Street parties' story has run on so long now, is it losing its power to shock? Has the understandable media preoccupation with Ukraine defanged it as a political risk to Johnson's position? Maybe. But at the heart of it lies something truly alarming and deeply profound. It's this:

When Boris Johnson rises to his feet at PMQs on a Wednesday to take a question on the *Ministerial Code*, the British constitution shudders. For its protector-in-chief has become its principal degrader in a grotesque reversal of the duties of a British Prime Minister. The constitution is unsafe in his hands. He has no feel for it in his mind and no love for it in his heart. It could still, in the end, be his downfall.

Diaries – famously – can be bringers of catharsis, receptacles of rage so hot that it singes the page, flowing out of the pen in an inky equivalent of molten lava. The most magma-like entry I have ever penned erupted like a burst of political vulcanology in the week before Easter 2022:

TUESDAY 12 APRIL 2022 WILL BE FOREVER REMEMBERED AS A
DARK, BLEAK DAY FOR BRITISH PUBLIC AND POLITICAL LIFE

It is the day Boris Johnson became *the* great debaser in
modern times of decency in public life and of our constitutional
conventions – our very system of government.

The moment was captured on film forever. (The story of
Johnson and Sunak's fines broke just before 1:00 p.m. on the
BBC). Just after 6 p.m., Johnson in a panelled room at Chequers
clutching a prepared statement which he read to camera for
Vicki Young of the BBC. He apologises, says he's paid the fine and
refuses to resign.

He was, he added, speaking 'in a spirit of openness and
humility'. If there were cocks on the Chequers Estate, they would
have crowed their very loudest at this point as the Prime Minister
sealed his place in British history as the first lawbreaker to have
occupied the premiership – an office he has sullied like no other,
turning it into an adventure playground for one man's narcissistic
vanity.

Boris Johnson has broken the law, misled Parliament, and, in
effect, shredded the *Ministerial Code*, part of the spinal cord of
the constitution, whose central organising principle is that you
do neither of these things, and that if you do, you go. The great
weakness of the system is that the Prime Minister (the wrong
'un-in-chief) is the guardian of the code and, with it, the supposed
protector of accountability and decency.

THE QUEEN'S FIRST MINISTER IS NOW, BEYOND DOUBT, A
ROGUE PRIME MINISTER UNWORTHY OF HER, HER PARLIAMENT,
HER PEOPLE AND HER KINGDOM. I CANNOT REMEMBER A DAY
WHEN I HAVE BEEN MORE FEARFUL FOR THE WELL-BEING OF THE
CONSTITUTION.

Johnson then deployed a pathetic litany of justification for his
behaviour on his birthday on 19 June 2020. The party had lasted
less than 10 minutes: 'It did not occur to me that this might have
broken the rules.' He said 'I fully accept the outcome of their [the

police's] investigation' – 'I want to be able to get on and deliver the mandate I have', when asked by Vicki Young if he was going to resign ...

THE BIG QUESTION IS HOW DOES PARLIAMENT AND THE COUNTRY COPE WITH A ROGUE PRIME MINISTER STILL IN PLACE AND WITHOUT SHAME IN DOWNING STREET?

On 14 April, Maundy Thursday, I record a piece for Paddy O'Connell's *Broadcasting House* during which I read the bulk of my diary entry for Tuesday the twelfth: 'I hope it doesn't sound too much like a despairing rant. It probably will.'

In the event, my Easter tirade probably had more impact than any broadcast I have ever made. Paddy said later that morning when we talked on the phone: 'You stepped into the carnivorous.'* Guto Harri, Johnson's press secretary, on holiday in Egypt at the time, had rung Paddy after the programme to say: 'It's a shame Peter is so disillusioned.' Jacob Rees-Mogg said that I didn't understand the *Ministerial Code*.

In the following days there was quite a bit of coverage of my tirade. Pippa Crerar in Easter Monday's *Daily Mirror*, kindly describing me as 'one of Britain's most respected constitutional historians', wrote I had 'branded Mr Johnson a "rogue Prime Minister" unworthy of the Queen', adding that 'the usually mild-mannered crossbench peer accused Mr Johnson of "sullying" his office like no other, turning it into an adventure playground for one man's narcissistic vanity'.[57]

The columnists were sympathetic. In *The Times* on Wednesday 20 April, Danny Finkelstein agreed we faced a constitutional crisis.[58] The same day, Marina Hyde in *The Guardian* quoted me quoting my diary:

---

* In his celebrated essay 'Festival', Michael Frayn made the distinction between 'herbivores' and 'carnivores' among the crowds at the 1951 Festival of Britain. See: Michael Frayn, 'Festival' in Michael Sissons and Philip French, eds, *The Age of Austerity: 1945–1951* (London, 1964), 331.

You don't need to be an esteemed political historian to work out that politicians defending prime ministerial lawbreaking will be doing something devastating and long-term to trust in the whole of politics. Then again, it does help to be one. On Sunday, the distinguished constitutional sage Peter Hennessy – not exactly given to intemperate public statements – declared of Johnson's failure to resign for breaking the actual law: 'I think we are in the most severe constitutional crisis involving a prime minister that I can remember.' Describing Johnson as 'a rogue prime minister, unworthy of [the Queen]', Hennessy went on to judge him 'the great debaser in modern times of decency in public and political life, and of our constitutional conventions – our very system of government'.[59]

As for the 'great debaser' himself, in the House of Commons on Tuesday 19 April, Caroline Lucas, the Green MP for Brighton Pavilion, put my 'rogue' prime minister line to him: 'I do not agree with that characterisation,' he replied.[60] Had he done so, it surely would have been the greatest surprise of Mr Johnson's career. The following day the prime minister flew to India. Speaking to journalists on the plane he said he would lead the Conservatives in the next general election. He could not think of any circumstance in which he would resign.[61] Time would tell.

4

The Twenty-Four Steps

Whatever is true, whatever is honourable, whatever is just, whatever is pure, whatever is pleasing, whatever is commendable. Think about these things.

Boris Johnson reading a passage from Philippians 4:8 at the Queen's Platinum Jubilee service, 3 June 2022

Maybe we're all deluded about our ambitions.

Boris Johnson before the House of Commons Liaison Committee, 7 July 2022

At first, I thought some brilliantly ironic Anglican wag in the deanery of St Paul's Cathedral had set up the prime minister in assigning him that passage from the New Testament to read at the Platinum Jubilee Service, given his current difficulties with all six 'things'. But a discreet inquiry revealed it was not so.[1] Pity. For if it were so, it would have taken the palm for the most sophisticated heckle in British political history – the dagger beneath the surplice.

There would have been justice in it, too. For Boris Johnson had always been a weathermaker politician in whatever context he was practicing his very personal version of the politician's craft. In the days after Easter '22, it was as if an especially malign weather system had somehow fallen upon the British Isles, trapped by Johnson's jet stream. The dominant question was: what would it take to shift it – and the prime minister with it?

The question of whether or not he had misled Parliament over those Downing Street parties haunted Johnson at every turn. On a visit to India at the end of April, Ben Wright of the BBC asked him: 'Did you mislead the House of Commons?' 'Of course not', he replied. With each denial Johnson's position weakened. His chief whip, Chris Heaton-Harris, told him he couldn't guarantee a Commons majority to defeat Labour's motion that there should be an inquiry into the alleged misleading by the House of Commons Privileges Committee.

I noted in my diary on 21 April:

This of itself was hugely significant as an indicator that once again Johnson's position within his own Parliamentary party is shaky ... But *the* gripping moment [in the Chamber] was Steve Baker [MP for Wycombe] withdrawing his support. 'The gig is over', he said. 'If the Prime Minister occupied any other office ... he would be long gone.' Very true.

Baker is a highly substantial figure – a man of real independent spirit. Given his [deep Brexiteer] politics nobody but nobody in Johnson's world can now claim it's all got up by disgruntled Remainers who have never accepted the referendum result. The debate ended without a vote. There will be a Committee of Privileges investigation. It will take a while, but Johnson is on the way out.

From India, the man himself declares he will still be prime minister in October.

When the great Johnson biography is written by a now young but by then middle-aged historian in the 2030s or 2040s, he or she will notice the phenomenon of political undertaking – a particular sub-branch of political sociology increasingly in play as his unravelling proceeded towards his demise, the hearse that carried an ever-greater collection of would-be morticians (or, better still, 'political coroners', as the great economic historian R. H. Tawney called them),[2] measuring Johnson up for his political coffin.

There is no doubt who would be in the driver's seat of the hearse – Johnson's old boss at *The Daily Telegraph*, Sir Max Hastings. His regular denunciations of his former Brussels correspondent saw passion jostling with eloquence. On 14 May, Hastings wrote, 'For the millions who mill in the middle ground, searching for hope, this can only be discovered in change. The only moral answer to the question "Who else is there?" is: "Anyone but Johnson."'[3] Would the Metropolitan Police inquiry aid Sir Max's cause? It still seemed possible when he penned his article in mid-May.

But, five days later, when the Met announced a final tranche of lockdown fines and declared that Operation Hillman was now at an end, Johnson's name was not on the list (nor was the Cabinet secretary's, Simon Case). A quick audit of Hillman is instructive:

Operation Hillman
Cost: £460,000
Fixed penalty notices: 126
Number of individuals: 83
Number of events covered: 8

This made Downing Street and the Cabinet Office the most Covid-fined part of the UK. Remarkable. 'Industrial-scale lawbreaking' as the former director of public prosecutions, Sir Keir Starmer, put it.[4]

Those on Johnson-watch now shifted their attention to 'Sue Gray 2' which was due to be published the following week. On Wednesday 25 May 2022 it came and the magma of outrage caught me in its heat once again. I tried to capture it in a long diary entry the following day:[5]

SUE GRAY or THE SHAMING OF THE PRIME MINISTER DAY
It was SHAMING – doubly SHAMING. Multiple SHAMING.
    The contents of the report are littered with debris: drunkenness (even vomit); disorderliness (a fight); and deception (instructions to keep bottles away from the camera and advice to leave parties by the back door).

Johnson's conduct of his defence in the House of Commons (deriding Keir Starmer for his 'sanctimonious pomposity')[6]* and his continued refusal to resign brought still more shame on him and another tranche of blight to the decencies and expectations of prime ministerial behaviour and the proper processes of central government.

As a result, the nation itself is shamed by having him as the Queen's First Minister – shamed both at home and abroad – and brought to a very low ebb, the lowest, in fact, that I have ever known.

Sue's report is the litany of a depleted nation, page after page after page of it [see sample in box] … A land of shame, no less, though it pains me to describe it thus.

SUE GRAY REPORT EXTRACT

[Exchange of emails on 17 June 2020 between two No.10 officials, relating to the 18 June 2020 leaving party for Lee Cain (No. 10 director of communications)]

'Hi Martin [Reynolds, principal private secretary] and Stuart [Glassborrow, his deputy] would like to do speeches tomorrow when we have your drinks which aren't drinks' …

'Well if we're doing it in Cabinet Room with a gap then to the actual drinks, I think we can more explicitly call it … goodbye or leaving speech, or something?' …

The event lasted for a number of hours. There was excessive alcohol consumption by some individuals. One individual was sick. There was a minor altercation between two other individuals.

The event broke up in stages with a few members of staff leaving from around 21:00 and the last member of staff, who stayed to tidy up, leaving at 03:13.[7]

The whole story is one of numbing awfulness; a dreadful

---

* Johnson's actual words were: 'And yet, after months of his frankly sanctimonious obsession, the great gaseous zeppelin of his pomposity has been permanently and irretrievably punctured …'

reflection of a superb country deeply diminished by the behaviour of its prime minister and the crawlers in the Cabinet who trot out the cardboard cut-out sentences No. 10 requires them to deliver at the first glimpse of a camera lens or the raising of a microphone. It is shaming, too, of the supine, duty-less Conservative backbench MPs who won't move against him.

The crucial question remains what it always has been – the lying to Parliament about the very existence of those Covid-busting parties. If the Commons Privileges Committee finds that Johnson knowingly did so, he will, at last, pass into the hands of the undertakers (i.e., historians like me). Or would he? Might he try and sit that out, too, refusing to relinquish the office to which he has brought so many patches of tarnish?

The Times' first leader caught it very well the next day: 'It is a sorry tale that will breed cynicism and draw contempt.'[8] A flavour of yet another dark day for political and public life:

KEIR STARMER IN THE HOUSE OF COMMONS
'This catalogue of criminality ... The values symbolised by the door of No. 10 must be restored.'[9]

AT THE 3:30 PRESS CONFERENCE
CHRIS MASON: 'Will you lie to get out of this?'

PRIME MINISTER: 'We all make mistakes. We will have to learn from them'.

BETH RIGBY asks him had he ever thought of resigning (she cites a new poll indicating that three out of five think he should).

PRIME MINISTER: 'It's my job to get on to serve the people of this country.'

PAUL BRAND: 'Are you a liar?'

PRIME MINISTER: 'No ... It really didn't occur to me that this was a breach of the rules ... My impression was I was at work events.'

On the ITV *News at 10*, 25 May 2022, Robert Peston describes the Gray Report as 'spectacularly damaging for No. 10 ... He will struggle to prove that he did not willingly lie [when he appears before the House of Commons Privileges Committee]'.[10]

On a personal note, I was much saddened during the week of Sue Gray's report when my former PhD student, Simon Case (to whom I had not talked, quite deliberately, for a long time to avoid embarrassing him) was the centre of a *Times* story on 27 May 2022 reporting significant disquiet among his senior civil service colleagues due to the fact that he had not resigned in light of the Gray reports (without any inside knowledge, I thought he would have 'walked', like an old-fashioned Test batsman, after the second one).[11]

Finally, to round off a truly dispiriting week, there occurred one of those changes to the British constitution that can strike many as immensely arcane but, at the same time, carries a powerful message about the very real fragility of said constitution if its supposed number-one guardian – the prime minister – is a wrong 'un.

At 'about 3:30 on a Friday afternoon, during Parliament's Whitsun Recess', I recorded in my diary:

> The Cabinet Office issue a new diluted version of the *Ministerial Code*. Gone from the PM's 'Foreword' are the words 'integrity', 'honesty', and 'transparency'. In comes a non-resignation tariff for transgressor ministers. Henceforth, the PM can call for an apology or drop a malefactor minister's salary for a bit. C. Geidt can initiate inquiries but only if the PM approves.
>
> It's hardly an act of contrition for the sins confirmed by Sue Gray. Did he think of how it would look? Did he care? Was it a

deliberately crafted taunt directed at the critics of his instinct for poor behaviour?

… More decencies consigned to the bonfire.

To his great credit, the Conservative chairman of the House of Commons' Justice Committee, Sir Bob Neill, came out against the changes in the Ministerial Code and revealed that he had sent a letter to Sir Graham Brady expressing no confidence in the prime minister (the public tally is now twenty-one).

On Sunday 29 May 2022, *The Observer* publishes an Opinium poll suggesting public opinion is hardening on the Johnson question. It found 56 per cent of all voters want him to resign and 32 per cent of those voting Conservative in 2019 wish him to go. The paper also carries a biting column by Andrew Rawnsley that touches on the 'good chap' theory:

> However long he hangs on to it, we can already be clear about one of the defining legacies of his premiership. It is the dustbin of history for the 'good chap theory of government'. The phrase was minted by Peter Hennessy, the eminent historian,* to describe the belief that Britain could get by with unwritten conventions about how politicians should behave, rather than a firm set of rules, because our politics was populated with honourable characters who could be relied on to do the right thing. If that theory were ever true, it has been tested to destruction by the rogue who is still squatting at Number 10 despite being a law-breaker who has repeatedly issued falsehoods to parliament. We now need to adopt a 'bad chap theory of government', which presumes that some politicians will behave abominably unless they are prevented from doing so by robust laws that are vigorously enforced.[12]

---

* Very kind – but its 'minter' was, in fact, Clive Priestley, an old Cabinet Office friend. I provided a kind of megaphone for it.

Much as I admire Andrew, this strikes me as defeatist. The decencies can be restored. A new prime minister could, within minutes of crossing the No. 10 threshold, set a new/old tone carrying real powers of restoration. Neither virtue nor poor behaviour is fixed in Whitehall. An expectation of the decencies, however, is. And, at the apex of politics and administration, it is indispensable. We know Johnson has transgressed these. We were warned from all sides that he would. And he did. When he finally goes, he will be the lodestar of how *not* to do the job of prime minister.

The day after Rawnsley's piece appeared, a former Conservative attorney general, Jeremy Wright, was eloquent about the Johnson effect on our institutions. In a 2,000-word blog, he declared that the lockdown parties had 'done real and lasting damage to the reputation not just of this Government but to the institutions and authority of Government more generally'.[13]

The next few days proved critical for the Johnson premiership. Influenced by the difficulty of shifting a prime minister who doesn't want to go, the daily barometer of my diary was still reflecting the volatile political weather that the destabilising of a PM brings:

TUESDAY 31 MAY 2022

Matters appear to be shifting against the Prime Minister. Andrea Leadsom writes to her constituents in highly critical terms of Johnson. WATO [BBC Radio 4's *World at One*] says 40 Conservative MPs are now publicly questioning his leadership. William Hague this morning tells Times Radio 'they are moving towards having a ballot … by the end of June … It strikes me the tilt is underway – we are seeing the UNMAKING OF THE PRIME MINISTER' [my capitals].[14] William Hague's intervention really counts.

With hardly a pause that Tuesday in late May, the chasm widened still further beneath Johnson.

Late afternoon, THE GEIDT MOMENT breaks. It is hugely

significant. Christopher has used his annual report as the PM's Adviser on Ministerial Interests to plunge deep into the heart of the matter using his devastating 'Preface' as his scalpel.

Here are a few flashes of Lord Geidt's dazzling blade work, in what historians may treat as a classic example of the 'good chap theory of government' striking back, as he dissected the events that 'could only risk placing the Ministerial Code in a place of ridicule ... the Prime Minister should be ready to offer public comment on his obligations under the Ministerial Code, even if he has judged himself not to be in breach.' He went on:

> The Independent Adviser is neither the author nor the guardian of the Ministerial Code. Those roles properly belong to the Prime Minister. Nevertheless, it is reasonable for the Independent Adviser, consistent with ... the Seven Principles of Public life, to promote the integrity of the Ministerial Code and ensure that its provisions are applied fairly and transparently.[15]

It turned out that Geidt had met Johnson that very morning. In the afternoon, the prime minister did attempt to justify himself in a letter to Geidt. In this letter, he tried to imply that his 'intent' – in other words, his wilful ignorance – cancelled out his actions. I penned: 'If a PM did not intend to breach the code then he was not in breach of it. THE BONFIRE OF ANOTHER DECENCY.'

There was, wrote Johnson in his letter to Geidt, 'no intent to break the regulations; at the time I did not consider that the circumstances in which I received a fixed penalty notice were contrary to the regulations'.[16]

That evening on *Channel 4 News*, the former Conservative attorney general, Dominic Grieve, described Johnson's reply to Geidt as 'a mealy-mouthed dishonest letter that completely flies in the face of the evidence ... He is a person who is completely shameless. His fingers are going to have to be prised off the window ledge'.[17]

We learned from *The Times* the following day that Geidt had threatened to resign at his meeting with Johnson if the prime minister did not issue a public explanation of his conduct in relation to the *Ministerial Code*.[18] Having been forced by his independent adviser of ministerial interests to make a public defence of his stewardship of the decencies, Johnson the day after was obliged to do the same in an interview with the admirably forthright Justine Roberts, founder of Mumsnet:

ROBERTS: [quoting a Mumsnet user] 'Why should we believe anything you say when it has been proven that you're a habitual liar?'

JOHNSON: Well, first of all, I don't agree with the conclusion ... that the questioner asked ... but look, er, I think the best way for me to answer that is to say, look at what I get on with and deliver, and what I say I'm going to deliver.

He told her he attended as 'we had to keep morale high, and the whole place was under a huge amount of pressure.' The whole thing had been 'a totally, you know, miserable experience'.[19]

Throughout what Boris Johnson rightly called this 'totally ... miserable experience', there ran a vivid contrast between two figures of public life – the head of state, Queen Elizabeth II, on the one side, and the head of government in the shape of Boris Johnson on the other. The first a pure-gold standard, the second akin to the basest of metals. Sir John Major, a highly decent man, highlighted this contrast while speaking on *Today* at the start of the Queen's Platinum Jubilee weekend. Sir John's interventions are always worth waiting for. This one was to be savoured especially, as I noted in my diary for 3 June 2022: 'John Major superb on TODAY. Speaks of HMQ's "decency" and devotion to duty. He needed no more to draw the stark contrast with her Head of Government.'

The poignancy of the platinum celebrations was deepened by the fragility of the Queen's health:

THURSDAY 2 JUNE 2022

TROOPING THE COLOUR on a bright shiny morning on Horse Guards Parade – the seven regiments of the Household Division glorious in their scarletry. B Palace appear to have been briefing on the symbolism of the Prince of Wales standing in for HMQ in taking the salute as yet another signal of the transition underway … 'Scipio', 'The Slow March of the Grenadier Guards' … Timeless Britain on the move. Pure balm – the contrast of tradition and orderliness with the chaos brought by the … 55-year-old in a morning suit sitting in the stands …

The Queen came on to the balcony supporting herself with a shepherd's crook as the propellers and the jet engines of the RAF did their stuff above … during the afternoon we learnt that the Queen would not be attending the service in St. Paul's tomorrow morning as she had experienced some 'discomfort' standing on the BP balcony for so long this morning. It was described as an 'episodic problem'. I profoundly hope it's no more than that.

FRIDAY 3 JUNE 2022

THE QUEEN'S PLATINUM LONG WEEKEND (SO FAR) It's an example – on a grand scale – of what Martin Charteris* once described to me as her extraordinary 'tonic' quality – a demonstration of the requirement of being CHEERER-UP-IN-CHIEF (and my, how we need cheering up).

On that theme, Boris Johnson was booed this morning when he climbed the [24] steps of St. Paul's with his wife for the Platinum Jubilee service. It was as if they (and, with them, a large part of the country) had rumbled him as a man with no *noblesse* and no *oblige*. Another step in the unmaking of the Prime Minister?

It was certainly a moment of considerable significance (or moments plural, to be precise, as the Johnsons were booed too as they came out afterwards and walked down the steps).

* A former private secretary to the Queen.

Danny Finkelstein wrote a fascinating 'Analysis' in *The Times* about the booing of the PM with something of a Bagehotian flavour about it:

A country that celebrates the Platinum Jubilee of a dignified monarch wants a dignified prime minister who respects the law and the office – and doubts that it has one.

Which is why one other aspect of today's event will worry No. 10. Booing is contagious.[20]

This is how *The Times'* reporters depicted the scene on the cathedral steps:

The boos and jeers were unmistakable as he walked up the stairs, hand in hand with his wife, Carrie. They did not react. The noise was loud enough for the BBC to address it in its live coverage of the event. Jane Hill, the presenter, said: 'There is really quite a lot of booing actually ... a substantial amount.' A few cheers among the crowd could also be heard.[21]

Then, inside the cathedral, came the reading. Never did an epistle drip with such unintended irony as the words came forth from Johnson's mouth.

As for the twenty-four steps, I noted that 'those who came to honour the Queen and ended up booing the Prime Minister, they were no bunch of republican lefties of Trotskyite inclinations. Quite the reverse. If he's lost them Johnson has lost his premiership'.

As the weekend unfolded, I sensed something about the Platinum Jubilee that surpassed all the others of her reign:

I think it's this. It was for the Queen something like a preview of the wave of affection, admiration and gratitude that will mark – along with the sadness – of the days after ... we have lost her; not quite a dress rehearsal but more than just a glimpse or a preview.

Another positive of the Jubilee was that the Queen was able to thank people for their warmth, which, of course, she would not be able to do in the wake of her death. Just after 5 p.m. on Sunday 5 June, she came out to the balcony of Buckingham Palace to mark the end of the Platinum celebrations. In a message released just afterwards she combined a renewal of her 1947 twenty-first birthday vow to serve with praise for the 'togetherness' demonstrated by her people over the past few days:

> When it comes to how to mark seventy years as your Queen, there is no guidebook to follow. It really is a first. But I have been humbled and deeply touched that so many people have taken to the streets to celebrate my Platinum Jubilee. While I may not have attended every event in person, my heart has been with you all; and I remain committed to serving you to the best of my ability, supported by my family.

Then came the we-can-do-better-than-this-as-a-nation theme at which she has always excelled:

> I have been inspired by the kindness, joy and kinship that has been so evident in recent days, and *I hope this renewed sense of togetherness will be felt for many years to come* [my italics].[22]

In other words, these qualities were her legacy; they were a crucial element of her realm and that of her successors. 'The 4 days,' I wrote at the time, 'have been a great squirt of superglue for her kingdom.'

Meanwhile, in the mire of Johnsonian politics and its consequences, matters had not been static. In *The Sunday Times*' Platinum weekend edition, its political commentator, Tim Shipman, produced one of those 360° all-round looks for which he has become famous. He noted that:

- More than the required 54 letters had now been sent to Sir Graham Brady (as many as 67, according to some claims).
- The announcement of this may come tomorrow and the resulting confidence vote held on Wednesday.
- Up to 190 Conservative MPs could vote against Johnson (10 more than the number needed to oust him).
- The Conservatives are nearly 20 per cent behind Labour in Wakefield where a by-election is due on 23 June (the same day as the one in Tiverton and Honiton).[23]

Monday 6 June (the seventy-eighth anniversary of D-Day) dawned with me wishing:

> I could calculate how the boos and whistles for the Prime Minister on the steps of St. Paul's converted into letters to Graham Brady. They may well have been mind-concentrators, for just around 8 a.m. Brady put out a statement saying the 54 threshold had been reached and, therefore, a vote of confidence will take place this evening. Speaking on College Green shortly afterwards, he said he had told Johnson yesterday and that the pair of them had agreed the timetable for today.

Shortly before, Jesse Norman, a politician-scholar whom I greatly admire (he and Rory Stewart were the stars of the 2010 Conservative intake), had sent a searingly critical letter to the prime minister. Jesse ranged across the widest of canvases, telling Johnson that 'under you the Government seems to lack a sense of mission. It has a large majority, but no long-term plan', and savaging pieces of policy along the way (the 'ugly' idea of deporting asylum-seekers to Rwanda).[24]

The big question now was how long Johnson could last. In the morning, the political media's conventional wisdom was that he would survive the confidence vote but that the arithmetic of survival would be critical. As the day wore on, the political reporters picked up increasing anxieties among Johnson's inner circle that the rebels might get something in the range of 140–150 rather than the 100 or fewer that No. 10 were hoping for. During the morning, Johnson personally signed letters to all Conservative MPs telling them they had 'a golden opportunity' to put all this behind them. His aides and supporters toured the lobbies and the corridors of the Commons telling MPs he would stay even if he won by a single vote.

At four in the afternoon, Johnson met his parliamentary party in the Boothroyd Room of Portcullis House. He promised them tax cuts, told them there was no one to take over from him, seemed to say (accounts differ) that he would do it all again (i.e. hold staff leaving parties). Jesse Norman had denounced him in his letter for presiding over 'a culture of casual lawbreaking in No. 10' and said it was 'grotesque' to claim Sue Gray had vindicated him. Johnson promised to lead them to victory again ('the best is yet to come'). In the background, a Conservative civil war raged.

On the ITV *Evening News*, Robert Peston said: 'There is tremendous uncertainty.' If 120–150 vote against him he will survive – but he won't necessarily be there in a few months' time.

The voting takes place between 6 p.m. and 8 p.m. On the dot of 9 p.m., in Committee Room 14, Graham Brady declares the result:

Johnson wins 211–148
(59 per cent to 41 per cent of the 359 votes cast)

Johnson, looking white, puffy, and exhausted, with a No. 10 bookshelf as his backdrop, resorts to a kind of patter of desperation: 'As a government we can move on and get on with things people want.'

Asked if it was a good result, the prime minister replied: 'I think it is.' He went on: 'An extremely good, positive, decisive result ... we're going to bash on.'

Would he go for a snap general election? 'I'm not interested in snap elections.' His overall verdict? 'The moment is decisive and conclusive.'[25]

'I THINK NOT,' I wrote in my diary. 'It will rage on. Tim Montgomerie said of Johnson's premiership: "It's finished." I think that's right, too. But there is much *sturm und drang* to come in between.'

At about the time I was putting those thoughts on paper, the printing presses (as I still like to call them) of *The Times* were preparing to roll with William Hague's regular Tuesday column among their pages. In *my* pages I wrote: 'William is one of the few contemporary politicians who fully appreciate the power of the pen' and this 'may turn out to be one of the most important political columns of modern times'. The gist of it is that Johnson's position is unsustainable, and he should seek an honourable exit and spare his party and the country further agony:

> If, with all the power of the party leadership, all the years of acquaintance with MPs, all the knowledge they have of your abilities and plans, you still cannot crush a vote of no confidence by a commanding margin, then not only is the writing on the wall but it is chiselled on stone and will not wash away.[26]

Later, on 7 June 2022, Lord Hague told *Times Radio* that Johnson was 'driving along the M1 on two flat tyres'.

In a very visible sign of weakness, the prime minister invited the television cameras into the Cabinet Room to capture his opening remarks to the meeting: 'To the accompaniment of little outbreaks of the nodding-dog phenomenon, he tells them last night's result was "decisive"; that "we're able now to draw a line under the issues our opponents want to talk about".'[27]

Wednesday at noon saw a Prime Minister's Questions positively dripping with hubris. Johnson claimed that Monday evening's vote by the 1922 Committee had left 'not even a flesh wound' and that his premiership had 'barely begun'.[28] More – much more – to the point was a letter as terse as it was apt in that morning's *Times*:

Sir, All I want in a PM is someone who is not a serial liar, has a mastery of detail and (perhaps I'm being a bit picky here) is not a serial womaniser. Surely that is not too much to ask.

ELIZABETH BALSOM
LONDON SW15[29]

It most certainly isn't.

A remarkable week ends with a remarkable piece of journalism. On Friday 10 June, Jesse Norman explained for the readers of the *Financial Times* why 'on Monday morning I found myself in the very distressing position of publishing a letter of no confidence in the prime minister, Boris Johnson, a man I have known and greatly liked for more than 40 years'.[*]

Norman took the Johnson debate to an altogether higher level: 'My objections are not restricted to the recent scandals of partygate, but relate to a much wider range of serious concerns including policy, approach to government and treatment of the British constitution. All are contrary to a decent, proper conservatism.'[30]

Norman, author of a fine biography of Edmund Burke,[31] went on to describe 'the genius' of the man who, in the late eighteenth century, was

> to turn the previously seditious language of faction into an understanding of political parties inspired by known and declared governing principles ... in parallel, there also re-emerged the ancient idea that a well-functioning political system should not have to rely on the character of virtuous leaders, indeed perhaps even be immune from that requirement. David Hume wrote of 'civilised monarchies ... that they are a government of laws not of men'.

---

[*] I don't share the national fixation with Etonians, but it should be noted that Johnson and Norman attended Eton College. The differences between the two men show just how futile it is to treat the breed as if they shared marked characteristics, one being a true scholar and a gentleman – the other not (for all his deployment of Latin tags).

British politics, Norman went on,

> has long been subject to what Peter Hennessy has called the
> 'good chap' theory of government. The effective working of the
> constitution has relied on leaders who, if not exactly virtuous,
> would respect and abide by the thicket of unwritten norms, rules
> and conventions that surrounded them. Of course this is an una-
> shamedly narrow, small-c conservative and, in some respects elite
> approach to government. But it has proven to be remarkably
> resilient and effective.

As for Johnson,

> It is as though the prime minister and some of his senior col-
> leagues have declared themselves exempt from the obligations of
> the good chap theory, but without any validating wider mission
> or purpose. Individualism in government has been purged of any
> connection to the local, the social, the greater public interest,
> and exists merely in the discharge of its own vanity. Yet the whole
> point of politics – and perhaps especially conservative politics
> – is to use power in the service of vital and enduring political
> principles.

'What, then, is to be done?' asks Norman. A *very* great deal is
his answer:

> [this moment] We must use it to rethink the basis of a proper 21st
> century conservatism. That starts with the great thinkers, Aristo-
> tle, Burke, Adam Smith, Hegel, Oakeshott. But it will need to
> engage with the great challenges of our time: of climate, race,
> inequality, war and peace, the balance between the generations.

That is a huge prospectus – and deeply long-term. Jesse Norman
rounds off his remarkable personal manifesto with what the coming

generation can realistically attempt (it's quite plain that nothing can now be hoped for from Johnson and his generation).

We need, Norman concludes, to 'look at ways to boost the evidently dwindling power of our political and constitutional norms, both in and outside parliament. With luck, one of its fruits will be a renewed public understanding of the best of our civic values and our history. Real leadership from a future occupant of Number 10 would help'.[32]

I hope future British political historians will linger a while, amid their coverage of the technicolour disintegration of the Johnson premiership, to savour the thoughts of Jesse Norman, who had served as a middle-ranking Treasury minister in Johnson's government and plainly come to realise its inadequacy and the impoverishment it had brought to what he called 'our political and constitutional norms'. Whether or not the British conservative tradition can find us another Burke or Oakeshott remains to be seen. But a party leader who is *not* tone deaf to the decencies of our wider political and governing traditions and the institutions that embody them is an immediate question. Much will turn on the man or woman who succeeds him and the degree to which they signal to us on day one that where government and decency meet, they will be anybody but Boris.

Meanwhile, one of the great possessors of those decencies, Christopher Geidt, continued to remind us of how short the prime minister had fallen in terms of the behavioural norms of the 'good chaps' tradition. Appearing before the House of Commons Public Administration and Constitutional Affairs Committee on 14 June, Lord Geidt said: 'It's reasonable to say that perhaps a fixed penalty notice and the Prime Minister paying for it may have constituted not meeting the overarching duty of the Ministerial Code of complying with the law.'[33]

'Must be a runner in the "understatement of the year stakes",' I wrote in my diary. 'In fact, he's a sure winner. The courtier had very definitely skewered the cad.'

The next day Lord Geidt *did* resign. The last straw seems to have been, of all things, the legality, or otherwise, of tariffs on steel – *not* Downing Street parties. The government had been seeking Christopher's guidance in advance on whether or not their steel tariff plans breached international law which, Lord Geidt described in his resignation letter, as 'a deliberate and purposeful breach of the Ministerial Code.' This, he wrote, put him in an 'impossible and odious position'.[34] No. 10, for its part, let it be known that Johnson was considering abolishing the job of adviser on ministerial interests altogether.

The courtier-versus-the-cad match seems to have attracted still more attention from the commentating classes. On Friday 17 June, Andy Marr rings to tell me he will announce the demise of the 'good chap' theory in his column in that weekend's *New Statesman*, which reaches me the following day. He writes:

> In London we have a less encoded political system than in Washington D.C. It is now too informal. Peter Hennessy's 'good chaps' theory of government has been shredded. From the Government's attempts to seize control over the Electoral Commission to the rewriting of the ministerial and parliamentary codes, we must fight for those slim and rickety barriers wo do have. I am becoming a little alarmed that the constitution – the rules of the game – are so little discussed by the opposition.[35]

Andy is right. Johnson has shown just how 'slim and rickety' our defences are.

More obsequies for the 'good chap' theory from the priests and priestesses of columnar come calling. On Monday 22 June in *The Times*, Clare Foges, after outlining Johnson's assault on the 'good chap' theory, argues that the prime minister has unleashed its rival – the 'great man' theory – and that the collision has killed it ('the "good chap" has been taken outside, beaten, strangled, and shot for good measure'). Yet she buys my and Andrew Blick's line that restoration is possible post-Johnson, quoting me in my Easter tirade about needing to codify 'in cold hard prose' more of the constitution with a royal commission or a cross-party inquiry 'to work out how to more clearly define key constitutional principles, and how they might be enshrined or defended'. In a rousing finale, she declares: 'Voters of Honiton and Tiverton: your country – and your constitution – needs you.'[36]

They – and the electors of Wakefield – did their duty three days later:

FRIDAY 24 JUNE 2022
Wake up to find Tiverton and Wakefield have done their stuff –
both barrels into Johnson. In doing so they [the bullets] passed
through the [Conservative] Party Chairman, Oliver Dowden,
who resigns at 5:35 this morning. What damage their flight will
do to the 'Big Dog' in Kigali [Johnson was in Rwanda for the
Commonwealth Heads of Government meeting] remains to be
seen. At the very least it will be considerable – maybe even fatal.
The PM is out of the country for eight days at various international
meetings. Even this most supine and meagre of Cabinets could
move against him in that time. Surely that 30% swing in Devon
should be a mind-concentrator even in 'this Cabinet of feebles', as
Mark Fox [businessman, political analyst, and former Conservative
parliamentary candidate] calls them.

Here are the voting figures that gave those Cabinet ministers their ordnance, if only they could bring themselves to detonate it:

WAKEFIELD
LAB MAJORITY 4,925
12.7% SWING FROM CONSERVATIVE TO LABOUR

TIVERTON AND HONITON
LIB DEM MAJORITY 6,144
29.9% SWING FROM CONSERVATIVE TO LIB DEM

The Tiverton swing was the largest ever in a UK by-election. Johnson, in Kigali, says: 'I've got to listen to what people are saying ... We will get through this.'

All Friday morning, the political electricity crackled. Would other Cabinet ministers follow Dowden's lead? Much was made of Dowden's resignation letter expressing his loyalty to the Conservative Party. On loyalty to the prime minister, the letter was silent. 'Somebody must take responsibility,' he wrote pointedly.[37]

Michael Howard, asked if Johnson should stay as party leader by Jonny Dymond on *World at One*, replies:

> I've very reluctantly come to the conclusion that he shouldn't. The party and, even more importantly, the country, would be better off under a new leadership. I don't think it's very likely that he will [resign]. It's not a step I have taken lightly ... Members of the Cabinet should very carefully consider their positions.[38]

Michael Howard added that he believed the 1922 Committee should amend its rules about annual leadership elections. Another former party leader, William Hague, echoes Michael Howard on the need for Cabinet ministers to consider their positions. 'Electoral disaster' awaits the Conservatives if Johnson stays.[39]

From Kigali? More defiance. 'No doubt people will continue to beat me up,' Johnson tells a press conference. In a long interview for *Channel 4 News*, he refuses to acknowledge that Sue Gray did *not* vindicate him.

On Saturday morning on the *Today* programme there is a highly interesting down-the-line between Mishal Husain in London and Johnson in Kigali:

> JOHNSON: If you want me to undergo some kind of psychological transformation ... that is not going to happen ... when you're in my job, you have to focus on what is right for the country.

HUSAIN: Is leadership about morality?

JOHNSON: Of course.[40]

Johnson claimed the voters were 'fed up with hearing conversations about me'. I think not.

No 'psychological transformation'. Is this the nearest we are ever going to get to a *public* admission of his *private* recognition that he's simply not suited by character, temperament, and configuration of mind to be prime minister?

Reading any prime minister's mind is a tricky trade, even, I suspect, if one is prime minister oneself. Whatever the motivations flashing around his synapses, Johnson gave an extraordinary interview before leaving Kigali for the G7 summit in Germany, as I recorded in my diary on 25 June 2022:

> He says he's thinking about policies for his 3rd term (which would take us up to 2029 and beyond). Later, No.10 says it was meant to be a joke. If it wasn't, it's 'white coats' time. How I hope Cabinet ministers are following the Hague/Howard advice this weekend and thinking how best to form up into a phalanx that will get Johnson out of No.10.

When the details came in of what he'd said in Kigali, it was quite plain that Johnson was *not* joking. It rang like a peal of bells: a mixture of boosterism, defiance, and self-delusion:

> At the moment I am thinking actively about the third term and you know, what could happen then ... We've embarked on a massive project to change the government, of the constitution of the country, the way we run our legal system, the way we manage our borders, our economy. All sorts of things we're doing differently. We also, at the same time, are embarked on a colossal project to unite and level up ... It's going to take time.[41]

Six days later, the name of Chris Pincher – the government's deputy chief whip – flickered across the pages of my diary. I gave him but a single sentence:

> **FRIDAY 2 JULY 2022**
> Johnson suspends Chris Pincher from the Conservative Party after No.10 spent much of the day saying the matter was closed and he would remain an MP.

Mr Pincher, it was being claimed, had made inappropriate advances to two men while in drink at a private party in the Carlton Club. The following day, Pincher says he is getting 'professional medical support' and hopes to resume his normal MP's duties.

The Pincher storm gathered force over the weekend as it increasingly played into the question of Johnson's wider judgement, as so many things did.

> **MONDAY 4 JULY 2022**
> PINCHER AFFAIR: No.10 admits Johnson *did* know about Pincher but his promotion to Deputy Chief Whip went ahead because there were no formal complaints at the time ... 14 more allegations have been made about him.

Suddenly, a drunken grope at the Carlton began to morph into the final phase of the Johnson premiership at a breathtaking pace, with Pincher's appetites as the trigger and the jagged relationship between Johnson and truth-telling as the propellant.

> **TUESDAY 5 JULY 2022**
> Dramatic moment on the TODAY programme. Simon McDonald, ex-PUS at the FCO, comes on to say Johnson *was* briefed in person on the outcome of [a previous investigation of Pincher when he was a Foreign Office minister] ... Of No.10's claims, Simon says: 'Not true ... I think they need to come clean.' He [McDonald] is

writing to the Parliamentary Standards Commissioner. Another
'good chap' who can take no more deceit. Raab follows him on
TODAY. Of Johnson's 'in person' briefing, Raab says, 'that's news to
me' (Raab was foreign secretary at the time).

There is an emergency debate in the H of C. The hopeless and
hapless Michael Ellis from the Cabinet Office declares '… the
Prime Minister acted with probity at all times.' No.10's new line is
that the PM did not recall this 'in person' briefing.

The demise of Johnson's premiership now took on an unstoppable
quality.

Suddenly it seems that there were others who could take no
more of Downing Street dissembling. Within ten minutes of each
other (and without collusion) just after Six, Javid and Sunak resign
loosing off highly damaging letters to Johnson just after Johnson
had called Chris Mason [the BBC's political editor] into the PM's
Room at the House of Commons to admit 'in hindsight', it was a
mistake to make Pincher Deputy Chief Whip.

Sunak compressed his case for the prosecution in a pithy two-sen-
tence paragraph:

The public rightly expect government to be conducted properly,
competently and seriously. I recognise this may be my last ministerial job, but I believe these standards are worth fighting for and
that is why I am resigning.[42]

Sajid Javid was more prolix but equally biting:

The tone you set as leader, and the values you represent, reflect
on your colleagues, your party, and ultimately the country.
Conservatives at their best are seen as hard-headed decision-
makers, guided by strong values. We may not always have been

popular, but we have been competent in acting in the national interest. Sadly, in the current circumstances, the public are concluding that we are neither. The vote of confidence last month showed that a large number of our colleagues agree. It was a moment for humility, grip, and new direction. I regret to say, however, that it is clear to me that this situation will not change under your leadership – and you have therefore lost my confidence too.[43]

Johnson had his defenders, among them Jacob Rees-Mogg, who took to *Channel 4 News* to do so. Jacob is 'a friend of mine', I wrote in my diary on 6 July 2022:

He has an unfortunate tendency sometimes to be loftily dismissive of other people which does not reflect terribly well on him. Of Sunak and Javid he said: 'They are eminently replaceable.' J said 'I'm supporting the Prime Minister who has a mandate from the British people ... I have no desire to serve another Prime Minister ... of course the Prime Minister tells the truth.'

Of Johnson's amnesia about his briefing on Pincher, Jacob said: 'It's perfectly reasonable to forget things.'

In his interview with Chris Mason, Johnson was asked: 'Can people trust you?' 'Of course they can,' he replied. A snap YouGov poll for Sky News suggested that is not how 'people' felt:

69% think Johnson should go.
54% of those who voted Conservative in 2019 think he should go.
21% think he will not go.
56% think Sunak was right to resign.[44]

So ended – or very nearly – an extraordinary day which, for Johnson, began with a prayer breakfast in Westminster Hall. It was here that the news of what Simon McDonald had said on *Today* was conveyed to him.

There was one epitaph on the day I really savoured – from Michael Heseltine, an old friend, who has long experience in such matters and was himself instrumental in Mrs Thatcher's demise in November 1990. On the ITV *News at Ten*, on the evening of 5 July, Michael predicted that Johnson would go 'sooner rather than later'. The Cabinet, he adds, are 'clinging like minor limpets' as they would not be members of anyone else's Cabinet. 'The PM will be told by enough senior people that the game is up.'

WEDNESDAY 6 JULY 2022
A DAY LIKE NO OTHER –THE GREAT GOVERNMENT BLEED-OUT

All morning the number of resigners mounted ... and rumours swirled that Gove had gone in to see Johnson to tell him to go. Javid delivers his biting resignation speech in the Chamber ('The reset button can only work a few times ... I have concluded the problem starts at the top and that it is not going to change.')

At PMQs, Starmer goes for the Cabinet: 'The Charge of the Lightweight Brigade ... Anyone with anything about them would have been long gone. A "Z" list case of nodding dogs'.

Early afternoon the number of resignations mount. There is word that Liam Fox has gone in to see him.

At 3:00 [p.m.] Johnson had to endure his long-awaited summer session with the Liaison Committee. As he took questions from the select committee chairs, the resignation tally rose and rose:

3:20	28
3:27	29
3:40	30
3:44	31
4:12	32
4:35	33
4:58	34

It was like keeping an eye on the Test Match score.

McNeil (SNP): 'Will you be Prime Minister tomorrow?'

PM: 'Of course.'

There is a fascinating, fleeting moment of self-awareness when Johnson is asked by William Wragg about his ability to find people to replace all the leavers. He tells Wragg never to underestimate the power of ambition adding 'Maybe we're all deluded about our ambitions.'

Wragg [Conservative chairman of the Public Administration and Constitutional Affairs Committee] raises the Lascelles Principles. Johnson seems to have heard of them but gets flustered when it comes to the detail. (The 1950 letter to *The Times* on the circumstances in which the Monarch can refuse a request from the Prime Minister to dissolve Parliament). Bernard Jenkin (in the chair) joins in trying to extract a pledge from Johnson that he won't cut and run for an election. Plainly there is worry that he might try to and, thereby, place the Monarch in a deeply difficult position and breaking the number one 'good chap' requirement that you don't embarrass the Queen by drawing her into political controversy. Johnson tells Wragg: 'You are asking me about something that is not going to happen ... You don't solve problems by threatening general elections.' He tells Bernard [Jenkin]: 'I see no reason for a general election.' So ended a rambling, distracted performance by the PM.

When Sebastian Payne, Whitehall editor of the *Financial Times*, published his book *The Fall of Boris Johnson* in November 2022, we learned that there were indeed serious worries within the innermost loop of 'good chap' circles.

Payne revealed that 'such were the fears within Whitehall that Johnson may do something reckless if his position was threatened that secret planning had taken place in the preceding months at the most discrete [sic] and deep levels of the British state, in case he asked the Queen to dissolve Parliament.'[45]

Payne checklisted the Lascelles criteria for a monarch refusing a dissolution request against the circumstances created by the crumbling of the Johnson premiership:

- The existing parliament was still vital, viable and capable of doing its job.
- A general election would be detrimental to the national economy.
- [The Monarch] could rely on finding another prime minister who could carry on [Her or His] Government for a reasonable period with a working majority in the House of Commons.[46]

Payne, rightly, judged that 'even during the chaos of Johnson's final days, all three of those conditions would have surely been met'.[47]

Payne's fascinating account added a new geographical expression to the cartography of the British constitution – the 'magic triangle' whose members, in the wild days of early July 2022, were the key guardians of the 'good chap' theory.

How, asked Payne, would the implications for the Lascelles principles have been communicated to Johnson? And who comprised the 'magic triangle'?

For the Queen to reject an election request outright would have prompted a full-blown constitutional crisis and have put the monarch in the most perilous position of her reign. One senior Whitehall figure said, 'It was a question that couldn't be put to the Queen because the Queen would have to say "yes". The PM cannot ask the question to which she ought to say "no" by the convention.' Instead, a 'magic triangle' of senior establishment figures had ensured it would never reach that point. Graham

Brady, representing the parliamentary Conservative Party, Simon Case, heading up the civil service, and the Queen's chief courtier, Edward Young had private channels of communication to ensure safeguards were in place.[48]

How would this very delicate operation have worked? Here is Seb Payne's depiction of the operation-that-might-have-been-but-never-was. According to a 'senior Whitehall insider', 'Tory MPs would have expected Brady to communicate to the Palace that we would be holding a vote of confidence in the very near future and that it might make sense for Her Majesty to be unavailable for a day.' Another senior official confirmed it would be politely communicated to Downing Street that 'Her Majesty couldn't come to the phone' had Johnson requested a call with the intention of dissolving parliament. One senior government figure said the 'magic triangle' had such a scenario mapped out. 'The Queen would never be asked a question to which she will say "no" to because the magic triangle will ensure that the prime minister doesn't ask.'[49]

Nicely done. The 'good chap' model still has wheels. Mercifully, Johnson did not pick up his phone, so the Queen did not have to pick up hers.

Back from the intensely private world of the 'triangle' to the very public events in Westminster. Never before had a British prime minister suffered such a slow and, by now, terminal crumble on television before a select committee. At 4:35 p.m. on 6 July, the BBC reported that a group of Cabinet ministers had gone to No. 10 to await Johnson's return from the Liaison Committee to tell him he had to go (chief whip, Zahawi, Lewis, Trevelyan, Hardy, Shapps). I wrote updates in my diary:

> 7:35 [p.m.] Reports that Patel has also told him to go.
> 7:55 [p.m.] Dorries leaves No. 10 saying she will stick by Johnson.
> A moment of sheer drama at 9:30 [p.m.] ... No.10 describes Gove as a 'snake'.

10:00 [p.m.] 1 in 5 of Johnson's ministers have resigned.

Even though I am at home, eight miles away from the mania and the frenzy, I succumb to it. At 11:45 p.m., I write 'a note to myself'.

> A hunch. PM behaved so oddly at the Liaison Committee and in No.10 this evening (sacking the 'snake' Gove) that he will be advised to see a doctor. Then what? Several days of complete rest advised. I really do think he's gone over the edge.

In fact, an hour or so before I committed that overheated thought to paper, Johnson had concluded the game was up. Seb Payne says he realised this when even loyalists like Simon Clarke could not be persuaded to replace Gove at the Department for Levelling Up. According to Payne, Johnson said: 'It's not fair on the nation to give them a D-list government.' He spoke his own epitaph: 'I can't do this, it's all too ghastly, it's not me.'[50]

THURSDAY 7 JULY 2022
THE DELUSION ENDS.
At 9:07 [a.m.], during the extended edition of TODAY, Chris Mason takes a call from No.10. He tells us Johnson had told Brady [at] about 8:30 [a.m.] that he is going to stand down. He would make a statement later outside No.10.

It instantly felt as if a heavy weight had been lifted. So much for what Johnson persisted in calling his 'colossal mandate' from the electorate. His government had melted – the heat of the meltdown had burnt off the delusion.

Yet, when it came, his speech at the No.10 lectern was long on defiance and short on humility. It was back to the scat-singing; the blaming of everyone else. Those who hold the eccentric view that he should go with a war in Europe; so much work to do on the economy. The 'herd', as he dismissively described his own MPs and Ministers had behaved as herds tend to do and moved;

he had been the victim of some 'pretty relentless sledging' ...
[There was] one flash of humility ('nobody is indispensable').
He would stay on until the Conservative Party has found his
successor.

An old and dear friend, a former Cabinet minister in the Major
years, Gillian Shephard, rings: 'The constitution took it. It worked.
We should be proud.' It *did* work – but my, how it felt a mighty
close-run thing.

On Friday morning, in a diary 'reflection', I asked myself:

What did the Johnson premiership teach us? Perhaps one thing
above all – just how vulnerable our deeply mature political system
is to the conduct of one person who is careless of convention,
probity and the decencies of public life; just how easy it is for a
prime minister to 'go rogue' if his Cabinet allows him to; just how
crucial are the duties of care prime ministers owe the constitution,
its 'tacit understandings',[51] and its codes.

We can no longer look upon our constitution as a flexible, self-
righting blend of instruments and expectations protected by an
array of checks and balances – a fortunate and highly favourable
gift of history, an accumulation of wisdom and experience all
based on a high sense of duty and restraint by those whose job
it is to 'work' the constitution [to use Gladstone's verb],[52] prime
ministers above all.

Will we, as a country, learn from this? What lessons should we
draw? What remedies should we seek? Will the candidates that
succeed him realise how crucial these questions are? Will their
'hustings' debates rise to the level required? Will the next prime
minister set out from day one to be anybody-but-Boris? Will the
Conservative Party selectorate even want them to? What might
happen to the country and the world while the contenders display
their prejudices for the approval of the 150,000-plus activists who

will determine which politician gets the next crack at the premiership? For the unmaking of Johnson had coincided with a menacing array of perils, from the mud of the Donbas through critical energy pipelines, fragile supply chains, and the multiple inflations roaring along the supermarket shelves.

Ukraine was a daily preoccupation throughout the frantic weeks of Johnson's undoing. President Zelensky deployed an unending stream of skilful public diplomacy. His armed forces showed themselves to be not just brave but highly adept at using their West-supplied precision munitions against the best the Russians could put in the field or in the air. Kyiv did not fall. The Russian advance was halted. Bit by bit, the Ukrainians retook territory. Johnson deserves credit for his unwavering political support and for the supplies of UK weaponry sent to the Ukrainian front line.

All these measures enjoyed cross-party support. But the rolling worries about an escalation of the war and, heaven forbid, the use of tactical nuclear weapons by Putin if he faced a humiliating defeat, all added to the recitative of anxieties that accompanied our daily lives in the spring and summer of 2022.

It was the strangest of times – a period of multiple uncertainties at home and abroad, most of which seemed way beyond the government-of-few-of-the-talents to handle let alone resolve as the contenders for the Johnson succession made their political calculations and prepared their pitches to the Conservative Party activists, in whose gifts of wisdom and discernment very few outside their own ranks had any confidence.

5

Hustings Inside a Heat Dome

The whole interminable farce has been largely, if not wholly, of
Johnson's own making. It is the ripest example of bad governance
in Britain since the war ... People may claim that Liz Truss was the
worst PM in history, but she was only a Boris Johnson tribute act.

Ferdinand Mount, *Big Caesars and Little Caesars*, 2023[1]

Sir Keir Starmer belongs firmly to The *Importance of Being Earnest*
school of politics. Not for him the flashing repartee of a Disraeli.
But at Prime Minister's Questions on Wednesday 13 July 2022, he
came up with this: 'The Prime Minister must be feeling demob
happy ... Finally he can throw off the shackles, say what he really
thinks and forget about following the rules!'[2]

The day before this probably well-rehearsed Starmerism, Sir John
Major, who can be a very witty man, had been at his most solemn
on the subject of prime ministers who break the rules during an
appearance before the House of Commons Public Administration and Constitutional Affairs Committee. He set the bar high
for Boris Johnson's successor and for those he or she recruits to
the Cabinet.

'The task for Parliament, the Government and this Committee,'
the former prime minister declared, 'will be to restore constitutional standards and protect from any further slippage against them
... Bad habits, if they become ingrained, become precedent. Precedent can carry bad habits on for a very long time, and it should not
be permitted to do so.'[3]

Sir John did not spare those who had fellow-travelled with Johnson and the Johnson style of government:

What has been done in the last three years have damaged our country, at home and overseas, and damaged the reputation of Parliament as well. The blame for these lapses must lie principally, but not only, with the Prime Minister. Many in his Cabinet are culpable too, and so are those outside the Cabinet who cheered him on. They were silent when they should have spoken out, and then they spoke out only when their silence became self-damaging.[4]

Sir John's draft history of the Johnson administration was swift and sharp. He struck me as a man who had been seething for all of those three years. It was also the critique of a fully paid-up subscriber to the 'good chap' theory of government, as this exchange with the chairman of the committee, William Wragg, illustrated:

WRAGG: You have referred to the delicate balance of respect for the laws made in Parliament, an independent judiciary, acceptance of conventions in public life and self-restraint by the powerful, upon which British democracy rests. What mechanisms exist to maintain that balance?

MAJOR: Self-restraint is, by definition, determined by the person themselves. It is self-restraint. There are no formal mechanisms to impose self-restraint upon Members of Parliament, civil servants or, indeed, anyone else. It is very difficult to see how you could actually do that ...

What helps self-restraint? Peer pressure undoubtedly helps it. The reaction to lapses of self-restraint will also be important. If somebody misbehaved in some way and there was a sharp reaction from their colleagues or from others, they might not be tempted to do it again. Traditionally, self-restraint has worked ...

The danger with breaking conventions is very real ... It devalues public life; it destroys the trust of the public in Parliament, which is a loss that is very serious, if it becomes sustained; it damages public faith; it undermines Parliament; it unsettles the constitution.[5]

'Unsettling the constitution' is as succinct a summary of the Johnson years as I have encountered so far.

How much did Sir John's thinking on constitutional matters play into the pitches the prime ministerial aspirants put together for their parliamentary party, then for the wider Conservative Party membership? It turned out to be a walk-on part at best. With one of them, not at all – as we shall see. It would be intriguing to discover if any of the candidates talked to John Major about it.

The 1922 Committee officers wanted a new PM in place in early September before the party conference met. Candidates needed at least twenty MPs to nominate them. On Monday 11 July, Rishi Sunak launched his campaign and talks of the need for 'honesty and responsibility, not fairytales' – a clever pitch that caught the anybody-but-Boris theme and rubbished Liz Truss's wishful thinking on the economy all in six words. Michael Gove, who had ruled himself out as a contender, gave an interview to Chris Mason on Tuesday 12 July that told us a good deal about the condition of the national political conversation:

MASON: Are you a snake?

GOVE: No ... I think I'm just a regular sort of guy.

At six that evening Graham Brady announced there would be eight runners in the Johnson succession sweepstake:

Nadhim Zahawi   Suella Braverman
Kemi Badenoch   Tom Tugendhat

| Jeremy Hunt | Liz Truss |
| Penny Mordaunt | Rishi Sunak |

There were to be hustings that evening (twelve minutes each) and Conservative MPs would ballot between 1:30 p.m. and 3:30 p.m. the following day.

On Wednesday morning, 13 July, Penny Mordaunt launched her campaign impressively at the Cinnamon Club: 'We have standards and trust to restore,' she said. Back in the wider kingdom, the Met Office issued an amber warning for the following Sunday, Monday, and Tuesday as the heatwave built.

At one minute past five, Graham Brady announced the result of the first ballot:

1st SUNAK	88	
2nd MORDAUNT	67	
3rd TRUSS	50	
4th BADENOCH	40	
5th TUGENDHAT	37	
6th BRAVERMAN	32	
7th ZAHAWI	25	} (out)
8th HUNT	18	

Both Sunak and Truss did less well than expected. Mordaunt, however, had momentum, with a YouGov/Sky poll suggesting she was the favourite of the wider Conservative Party.

The next morning, 14 July, Truss launched her bid. All politicians carry their own distinctive weather system around them. Liz Truss's had an uneasiness about it that felt even greater the more she asserted her qualities: 'I can lead. I can take tough decisions.' She would, she said, lead 'an aspiration government'. 'What she *didn't* do', I noted in my diary, 'was manage to create a sense of energy or occasion. She was late – missing [Kwasi] Kwarteng's cue. She was white-faced, tense, ill-at-ease and parts of her delivery faltered.' In what might later be seen as an omen of political defenestration-to-come by the politically superstitious, 'she left for what she thought was the door and turned out to be a window'.

At 3 p.m. Brady announced the result of the second ballot:

1st SUNAK	101	(+13)
2nd MORDAUNT	83	(+16)
3rd TRUSS	64	(+14)
4th BADENOCH	49	(+9)
5th TUGENDHAT	32	(-5)
6th BRAVERMAN	27	(out)

On the evening of Friday 15 July, as the five surviving runners prepared for the Channel 4 candidates' debate, the Met Office issued its first ever red weather warning for the next Monday and Tuesday. A great swathe of England, covering London and the Midlands, reaching north to Manchester and York, could see temperatures reach 40°C.

I reacted to Channel 4's debate in my diary:

Krishnan GM [Guru-Murthy] [says] 'trust' is by far the question most frequently asked. Tom T is the only one who replies unequivocally to K's question 'is Johnson honest?' T simply shakes his head and wins loud applause. Tom shines: 'Who are you serving? Your country or your career? I swore loyalty to our country [as a soldier] and I always shall.'

Penny M's words are good for the most part, but she lacks fire and did not dominate the room: 'I'm not a legacy candidate in this election.'

Rishi is full of vitality and pounces on his critics. He's particularly hard on Liz Truss and her 'fairytale economics'.

She (Truss) is tense, anxious, unsmiling. white-faced. Looks unwell and/or lacking sleep. Not a flicker of warmth. She does worst.

K Badenoch is confident. She could well be leader one day but won't make it this time. To the 'is Johnson honest?' question, she replies 'sometimes'.

The leadership contest has largely swept Johnson from the headlines which will, no doubt, be irritating him. But what a blessed relief for the rest of us.

The following day, the press pick up on Truss's homage to Mrs Thatcher in the shape of the great white bow she was sporting at the debate.

Sunday 17 July brings a temperature of 33°C to Hawarden on the Anglo-Welsh border near Chester, where Mr Gladstone used to live in Hawarden Castle, and the second debate, courtesy of ITN, airs at 7 p.m. I write in my diary:

Cost of living starts. They repeat their previous lines. Truss appeared more confident and fluent but still no warmth.

Character, honesty, and trust make up the second theme. One moment of electricity when Julie Etchingham asks candidates [if they were] willing to give Johnson a seat in their Cabinet if he wished to have one? Not one of the five raised their hands.

Johnson, who later was said not to have watched the programme, being a vindictive man who never forgets a slight, will not forgive those five who visited such a public humiliation on him.

The exchanges grew in brutality. Rishi Sunak was the chief object of the others' fire. This, I think, increased his status – and he did pretty well in his rebuttals.

Penny M did well when she emphasised her team approach: 'Our leadership model is completely broken.'

Tom T struck a blow against the others when he said 'even good people gave credibility to the chaos'.

Sunak asked Truss what she regretted most: having been a Lib Dem or a Remainer? She had, she said, been 'on a journey'.

Reflecting further on the candidates' debate, I noted that:

This was so raw and the dislikes so intense, it was, I think, a
spectacle that will do the Conservatives considerable harm during
the 'long election campaign' that will start the moment the new
PM comes before the cameras in Downing Street on 5 September.
There is something slightly mad about a Conservative micro-
world in which Sunak can accuse Truss of being a 'socialist'.

On Monday 18 July, Sunak and Truss *did* pull out of Tuesday's
planned debate because the first two had inflicted such damage
on the Conservative Party. As a result, Sky cancelled the event.
The heatwave continued to build. Luton Airport and RAF Brize
Norton closed as the runways melted. Hawarden reached 37.1°C (a
new record for Wales) and Santon Downham in Suffolk reached
38.1°C. The highest temperature recorded in the 1976 heatwave was
36°C.

'Britain,' I wrote in my diary, 'sits sweaty and uneasy beneath its
"heat dome".' The sense of heatstroke among the Conservative Party
also rises when Johnson makes a self-parody of a speech during the
confidence vote he has called in his own government ('the great
blue ferret up Labour's trouser leg').* Starmer says: 'The delusion
is never ending.'[6] Meanwhile, as Johnson hints at some kind of fer-
ret-led vengeance in the Chamber of the House of Commons, his
party continues to eat itself. There are rumours that Michael Gove
is some kind of Machiavelli manipulating Kemi Badenoch for his
own ends. Gove attracts these sorts of stories in the way Peter Man-
delson used to.

On Sky News that Monday evening, just before the result of
the third ballot was announced at 8 p.m., Michael Heseltine mixes
understatement with regret: 'The policy content of the leadership

* His actual words were: 'We sent the great blue Tory ferret so far up their left
trouser leg that they could not move.'

debates has been very disappointing,' he says. For example, they had hardly touched upon devolution.

THIRD BALLOT RESULT

1st SUNAK	115	(+14)
2nd MORDAUNT	82	(-1)
3rd TRUSS	71	(+7)
4th BADENOCH	58	(+9)
5th TUGENDHAT	31	(out)

Sunak was five short of the votes he needed to get into the wider party run-off.

Two hours later, the government won its confidence vote in the House of Commons, as expected.

TUESDAY 19 JULY 2022
'THE DAY OF THE HEAT DOME'
The day we watched the mercury rise on an upward trajectory of record-breaking.

NOON:	39.1°C,	CHARLWOOD (IN SURREY)
1 P.M.	40.2°C,	HEATHROW
4 P.M.	40.3°C,	CONINGSBY (IN LINCOLNSHIRE)

Even with all the advanced forecasting we'd received, there was still a burst of shock and alarm as the finger of heat coming up from the Sahara via the Iberian Peninsula put nearly 1 ½° on the previous record (CAMBRIDGE, 38.7°C, 2019) with the flaring-up of fires and the wilting of infrastructure across the nation in the humid heat … In England, over 34 locations surpassed the previous 2019 record. Network Rail issues a 'do not travel' warning and the East Coast Main Line is closed from Kings X to York and Leeds.

FOURTH BALLOT RESULT (4 p.m.)

1st SUNAK	118	(+3)
2nd MORDAUNT	92	(+10)
3rd TRUSS	86	(+15)
4th BADENOCH	59	(out)

8 p.m. IT STARTS TO RAIN! The new weather front is moving over. It's getting cloudy and the wind is picking up. Hooray! Like the country's infrastructure, I am not built for these temperatures.

The Met Office warns that we can expect heatwaves like this every three to four years.

That morning saw Johnson's last Cabinet meeting. He was presented with red leather-bound volumes of Churchill's war memoirs. Suella Braverman shed a tear.

Public Service Pay inserted itself into the nation's consciousness; offers to NHS staff, police, and teachers did not go down well. Was there yet more trouble ahead?

WEDNESDAY 20 JULY 2022.

Johnson's last PMQs. He enters the Chamber to cheers from his own side. In a nice touch, Speaker Hoyle recognises James and Beth Mackay in the Peers' Gallery [the universally admired former lord chancellor, James Mackay, having retired from the House that month aged ninety-three]. He then wishes Johnson well and mentions his conduct of the pandemic. He reminds members (vainly) that the session should be conducted without personal attacks. Starmer wishes Johnson and his family well. In return, Johnson attacks Starmer for opposing the lifting of lockdown. Starmer reminds Johnson of Sunak's words about 'fantasy economics'.

There followed one of those exchanges that makes one question the notion that the House of Commons is the most sophisticated legislature in the world:

STARMER: I am going to miss the delusion …

JOHNSON: He is a great pointless human bollard.

In a final crescendo:

Johnson attempted his own personal epitaph. It was 'mission largely accomplished'? And then: 'Hasta la vista, baby' [the meaning of which was quite lost on me – and had to be explained later].* His MPs stand and applaud but not – very pointedly not – Mrs Theresa May.

4 p.m. RESULT OF THE FIFTH BALLOT
1st SUNAK   137   (+19)
2nd TRUSS   113   (+27)
3rd MORDAUNT   105   (out)

The result of the membership ballot was to be declared on Monday 5 September at 12:30 p.m. The new prime minister would be appointed on Tuesday 6 September.

On 22 July I pen a 'reflection' in my diary:

There is a very strong chance with Sunak and Truss in the final run-off, tax will remain the pacemaker. It's morphing into two reheated versions of Thatcherism. I'm struck by the poverty of their inspirations. Can we discern the merest dash of originality in anything the pair of them have said? That Mrs T should still be the great political weathermaker for her party nearly 32 years after she left Downing Street is quite remarkable. There is a howling gap at play. Danny Finkelstein concentrates on it in his bitingly brilliant column in this morning's *Times*:

* In *Terminator 2*, Arnold Schwarzenegger says exactly that – meaning 'I'll be back'. Heaven forbid.

'Conservatives believe in the maintenance of the unwritten constitution and its conventions. Johnson's conduct in office was a more serious attack on the parliamentary tradition than has been achieved by most radical protest movements. Only at the very last moment did parliament move to reassert itself and insist on certain standards of behaviour. What sort of Conservative Party can have a leadership election and not discuss that?[7]

The answer is – 'our one'.

The following day YouGov published the first poll since the race was reduced to two. It put Truss 24 per cent ahead of Sunak, prompting me to write: 'It may not be on the Johnsonian scale, but Truss really has swallowed her legend whole. As for her own surpassing insights – she's vowed to overturn 20 years of economic failure. Rishi told Andy Marr on LBC he was offering "common sense Thatcherism".'

I have a chat with my old friend, Garry Gibbon, political editor of *Channel 4 News*, about the long shadow of Mrs Thatcher. Later he emails: 'I was just thinking ... how the great ghost of Thatcher has now seen the Tories splinter into rival presbyterian churches – one kirk says Mrs T's holy scripture was tax cuts, another that it was balancing books.' Spot on. Sunak's wife, Akshata Murty, is photographed taking a selfie in front of the new statue of Mrs Thatcher in Grantham.

Interestingly, in his column in the *New Statesman* the following weekend Andy Marr picked up the narrowing of UK politics and how this was mirrored in the political journalists' trade:

We often prioritise only what is happening now, and our political system reflects that. The parliamentary structure is the institutionalisation of prevarication ...

Climate change, species extinction, the consequences of global

migration, starvation, and the upending of the world order for
cosy little Britain are horrible issues to think about.[8]

In this article, Andy introduces a very useful new political concept
– 'sugar-rush politics'.

Sunak, to his credit, seemed to have sensed this mood and kept
stressing that the public must be told the truth about the multiple
crises the country was facing, promising a fistful of task forces if he
becomes PM, on the NHS treatment backlogs, inflation, and immi-
gration (he pledged to increase the speed and scale of the Rwanda
deportations – did he really believe this last undertaking or was he
trying to fireproof himself against the Rwanda enthusiasts in his
party?) Truss, for her part, picked at the Brexit scar, promising to
get rid of all residual EU legislation by the end of 2023.

SUNDAY 24 JULY 2022
Wild talk in the papers of rumours that Johnson is backing Truss
because she is so hopeless she'll implode in No.10 clearing the
way for him to return.[9]

Dom is imploding again. Have a listen to Andrew Rawnsley in
this morning's *Observer* on Truss:

Dominic Cummings, who has known her for a long time,
remarks: 'She's about as close to properly crackers as anybody I
have met in parliament.' He predicts that she would be an 'even
worse' prime minister than his former boss …

Mr Cummings has a conspiracy theory, which sounds so
wacky it could be true, that Mr Johnson reckons there's a good
chance she will blow up at Number 10, opening the door for
him to return.[10]

Such was the mania on the eve of the first Sunak/Truss debate.

MONDAY 25 JULY 2022

A biting email from Max Hastings: 'The Tories are about to achieve the miracle of appointing the only human being in Britain capable of governing worse than Johnson.'

I suspect (and fear) Max is right. How much of this would be apparent in tonight's debate … in the Victoria Hotel, Stoke-on-Trent …?

They began with a dreary reprise of their cost-of-living positions. RS went straight on the attack over her supporter, Patrick Minford [a monetarist academic who won favour with Mrs Thatcher], saying her tax cuts could lead to interest rates at 7%. She is quite shaky when drawn across the political economy terrain. RS was effective by linking the absence of 'morality' in passing debt to our children if you fall for the temptation of 'the short-term sugar-rush of unfunded tax cuts'. He was also much better on the *wider* ingredients of economic growth.

The atmosphere between them was pretty caustic. RS plainly believes she is not up to being PM. Niddy [Enid, my wife] notes how 'wooden' Truss comes across. She comes over as vain, too, regularly reminding us how brilliant she has been at trade deals and being Foreign Secretary. She is high up the scale of political and personal self-delusionists. RS says his first job as PM would be to restore trust and integrity …

In terms of fitness for the job, he is streets ahead of her. But, I fear, this is not how it will turn out. The Conservative Party this time will give the country a vain mediocrity. Last time they gave us a narcissistic nightmare – unless Truss implodes in some way or another in the next 4+ weeks.

Another factor in the swirling plasma of Conservative emotions in that sticky summer of 2022 was absorbing the significance of the Johnson premiership. Some reports suggested that about 10,000 of the party's members wanted him to remain as PM. What more did he have to do to demonstrate his unfitness for the highest office?

There was a whiff of this in William Hague's column in *The Times* on 26 July. 'Some former PMs,' he wrote, 'have good cause to attack disloyalty, but in Johnson's case the disloyalty was his own – to the conventional institutions of government and to the massed ranks of colleagues who did their best to support him but ultimately quit in disgust or told him to go.'[11] Later in the week, James Mackay said it all with his characteristic verbal economy: 'People have forsaken him [Johnson] for not sticking to the rules – he hasn't bothered with them, or with respect for truth and integrity.'[12]

On 31 July, the eve of the ballot papers going out to the Conservative Party membership, I scribble: 'Mood in the press is that Truss has it in the bag. 5 more bloody weeks to go.' Johnson, at his delayed wedding reception in the Cotswolds, tells his family and friends the day his ministers deserted him in droves was 'the greatest stitch-up since the Bayeux Tapestry'.[13]

On the evening of 1 August, at a hustings meeting in Exeter, Liz Truss took my breath away with one of the most crass remarks of modern British politics: 'The best thing to do with Nicola Sturgeon is to ignore her.'

I could scarcely believe it:

It was rude, arrogant, insensitive, patronising, and counter-productive. You can't 'ignore' the First Minister of a constituent nation full-stop – let alone one whose party keeps winning elections in Scotland. It was deeply, deeply insulting. Ms Sturgeon is a far more astute politician than Liz Truss will ever be, and she will accumulate much political capital from this example of Liz Truss's tone-deafness. It is not – very much not – a way to save a Union. In saying that Liz Truss moved beyond her mediocrity and into the realm of the seriously harmful.

With a stunning lack of self-awareness, especially given her Thatcher-like posing on tank turrets and more, Truss denounced Sturgeon as an 'attention seeker'.

Two days later, she did it again. This time the target was one of the most gently agreeable people in UK politics, the Welsh first minister: 'We will be able to take on,' she declared, 'the low-energy version of Jeremy Corbyn that is Mark Drakeford.'[14]

At such moments, diaries are for shouting into:

She has probably never heard of Attlee's sage advice to Jim Callaghan when giving him his first ministerial post: 'Never insult a man today; you many need to negotiate with him tomorrow.' She *knows* she will have to negotiate with the Welsh First Minister at some point. That's how devolution works. What a narrow, meagre, partisan person she is. She strikes me as a Dorothy Parker politician (Parker's remark on Hollywood – 'there's no there there'). To insult two of the UK's nations in two days – what a brilliant stroke.

All this when we need a truly broad-gauge figure in No. 10 to cope with an ever-darkening economic scene. On 4 August, the Bank of England raised interest rates for the sixth consecutive time (by 0.5 per cent to 1.75 per cent) and dished out a grim set of forecasts:

- Inflation to reach 13 per cent early next year.
- Recession to start in the final quarter of 2022 and to last right through 2023.
- Average household energy bills to reach £3,500 that autumn.

It was, I noted,

the day the mood music, already jarring, changed very much for the worst – worse than anything we have experienced since the 2008 financial crash. Nearly all the old, familiar and ever-depressing threnodies are back accompanied by the usual mutual scapegoating. Andrew Bailey doggedly slogs his way through a series of interviews. The Conservatives (or some of them) mutter about cutting the Bank less slack and reducing its independence.

The shadow of a Truss administration fell evermore upon the kingdom and, diary-wise, on my desk.

FRIDAY 5 AUGUST 2022

As the prospect of a Truss premiership in almost exactly a month's time looms, thoughts, and speculations, begin to trickle between the synapses. In a struggle to find reasons to be cheerful, there is undoubtedly one: she is *not* Boris Johnson. She showed real insensitivity towards the British constitution when Lord Chancellor and tardy to come to the defence of the judiciary when the *Daily Mail* described them as 'enemies of the people'. But she is not, I think, a serial rule-breaker or convention-buster.

But when one considers the almost Himalayan range of problems she will face on 6 September, her problem is of mediocrity, narrowness of range, meanness of spirit, profound unoriginality combined with considerable reserves of self-belief. All these deficiencies could be cruelly exposed long before Christmas. She is a diminisher of political life, not an enhancer.

I've just re-read Blair Worden's review of Douglas Hurd's biography of Robert Peel … 'Like Attlee or Thatcher, he [Peel] stamped the future.'[15]

Johnson's 3 years *did* stamp the future as did Ted Heath's 3¾ years because of Europe (the engineers of exit and entry respectively). But a 'Truss-ism' that changes our political economy or a 'Truss settlement' which extends the duties of the state and moves the political centre of gravity – I think not. As for the wider appeal of her public character (a whiny tendency to self-righteousness and preachiness) – not attractive. As for her remarks this week about Sturgeon and Drakeford, the Union is very definitely *not* safe in her hands.

The value of the diary as a necessary humbler of the diarist was very evident on 5 August when, gloom getting the better of me, I offered a forecast which (I'm glad to say) proved wrong:

> The word is that a Truss government will have an emergency budget on 21 September. Paul Johnson of the IFS points out that the leadership debate so far has avoided the things that most matter – public services investment and effective help on the cost of living. ONS reports that 24m of us are using less gas and electricity and that 16m of us are cutting back on food. I sense social unrest in September as well as an emergency budget. The drought-parched parks may be symbolic of a physical heatwave in Britain – but just one spark may be all it will take for the blue lights to flash, the sirens to wail and the riot shields to come up. The pathetic cries of 'tax cuts' and 'a smaller state' might do well in the back gardens of Tunbridge Wells,* but on the streets of the inner cities and the run-down council estates it will be the petrol bombs that take flight, not the thoughts of Truss and Sunak.

The impoverished debate tottered on. Saturday 6 August saw Truss declare: 'What I will do on day one is reduce taxes'; she did not believe in 'handouts'. She accused the Treasury of practicing 'abacus economics'. Sunak said that if the government cannot bring inflation under control, the Conservatives 'can kiss goodbye' to the next general election. As for the leadership contest, the choice, said Sunak, is between 'clear-eyed realism' and 'starry-eyed boosterism'.

The poverty of thought combined with crudity of analysis that is the Truss trademark had a depressing little outing on 10 August. Sunak said he felt 'a moral responsibility' to go further on help with fuel prices. His intention was to tell people what they needed to know rather than what they wished to hear: 'I would rather lose

---

* *The New Statesman* had acquired a video of Sunak speaking in just such a garden last week and telling his listeners how, as chancellor, he had shifted government funds from Labour-controlled areas to places like Tunbridge Wells.

than win on a false promise.' Truss accused him of having 'socialist principles'. Reality departed – if it ever were there.

The heat returned. On Thursday 11 August, the temperatures reached 34°C to 35°C in the south-east of England. The following day, an official drought emergency was declared in eight of the fourteen areas, Sunak saying that if he becomes PM he will borrow an extra £10 billion to assist the 16 million most vulnerable to energy price rises. There were reports of Johnson refusing to take calls from Sunak. The industrial unrest accumulated – ASLEF drivers would walk out on 12 August, affecting nine train operating companies; there were to be postal strikes at the end of the month.

How fared the emotional geography of the tiny Conservative Party selectorate who would give us our next PM? An Opinium poll in *The Observer* on 14 August put Truss 22 per cent ahead of Sunak among party members (61 per cent against 39 per cent). Conservative Party members appeared quite unrepentant about inflicting Johnson on us in 2019 – 63 per cent of them would have preferred him to carry on as prime minister.[16]

In the same paper, Will Hutton filled his column with despair over what a Truss premiership could bring. He asks his readers to

consider her six-point plan for growth. It starts, inevitably, with a commitment to cut taxes 'now'. She will 'unshackle' business from burdensome regulation buttressed by 'supply-side reform'. She will scrap all EU-derived laws by 2023 and 'work with industry leaders to regulate for British businesses and consumers'. She will 'create low-tax, low-regulation zones'. And she will revisit the Bank of England's mandate so that it is better at managing inflation. It is ruinous nonsense.

'Reality', Hutton declares, is not allowed a look in:

There is no recognition that what matters in a decade beset by a pandemic, climate breakdown, fragile energy markets and threats to food supplies is the resilience of a country's energy, public health, water, and farming systems to support business and civil society, in all of which the state has to apply a leadership role. There is no comprehension that today's economy is built on the 'intangibles' of knowledge, intellectual property and digitisation for which smart regulation – not no regulation – is fundamental.[17]

On the constitutional front, Liz Truss announced that, like Johnson, she would make herself minister for the Union. Difficult, that one – especially if you won't talk to the first minister of Scotland (a neat, if depressing, example of Attlee's law).

There is a book to be written (though not by me) about how weather impacts on political mood. I offer an exhibit from the summer of Truss and drought:

TUESDAY 16 AUGUST 2022
To Orkney on the impossibly early 7 a.m. flight from City to Edinburgh … [over] the parched, yellow-brown fields beneath us … As we touch down at Edinburgh, I say to Niddy: 'Look through the window. That's called rain.' It pours as the kind wheelchair-man pushes me to the terminal – feel tempted to get out and lie in the biggest puddle I can find on the tarmac. As for the Northern Isles, the bright green landscape of Orkney is deeply beautiful as we come out of the cloud into the clean, rinsed air which is such a contrast from the muck we've been breathing trapped inside our heat dome down south.

Truss and Sunak were in Scotland, too, for a hustings beside the Tay in Perth. Both ruled out a second Scottish referendum. Truss said she would 'never ever' let the UK be split up. She would ensure the Union went from strength to strength 'now and forever'.[18] With every word, you could feel the bonds of the Union fraying.

The new political editor of *The Guardian*, Pippa Crerar, had a rich scoop in that morning's [Wednesday 17 August] paper. She had got hold of a leaked recording of Truss speaking when she was chief secretary to the Treasury. British workers, she said, 'need more graft'. They lacked the 'skill and application' of foreign rivals. It was, she said, partly 'a mindset or attitude thing' for areas outside London.[19] At least this shifted the leadership debate on to the big question and away from the tax discussion.

A touch old and a touch jaded as I am, I could never see the Truss prescriptions securing the productivity transformations that had eluded Cripps/Attlee; Rab Butler/David Eccles; Macmillan/ Maudling; Wilson/Brown; Ted Heath; Thatcher/Howe; Major/ Heseltine; Blair/Brown. Nor did I ever think she had the personality to move people. Even if she did have the 'market' impulse, I thought, she certainly had no feel for the 'social' bit of the social market. A successful economy needs both. I wondered if she had any idea of what Erhardism was about in post-war West Germany. And she was certainly no de Gaulle.

The Conservative civil war was feeding into the opinion polls. In *The Times* of Saturday 20 August a YouGov poll gave Labour a huge lead (LAB 43 per cent; CONS 28 per cent; LIB DEM 11 per cent; GREEN 7 per cent). In the same edition of the paper, its former employee Michael Gove accused the Truss camp of taking 'a holiday from reality' and warned that her proposed tax cuts would put 'the stock options of FTSE 100 executives' before the needs of the poorest.[20]

But the top billing in the 20 August edition of the paper was taken by Matthew Parris in one of the most brilliant polemical weapons he has ever fashioned in that ordnance factory of a mind:

> Liz Truss is a planet-sized mass of overconfidence and ambition teetering upon a pinhead of a political brain. It must all come crashing down ... I'll wager that at the outset most readers thought Liz Truss a bit weird, curiously hollow, and potentially dangerous. This summer a short period will see such rushes to

judgement revised. The government will descend into a huge effort to contain and defang an unstable prime minister, and we shall revert to our first impressions. Save yourself the detour and stick with them. She's crackers. It isn't going to work.[21]

If things did go wrong, Parris's fellow Conservatives could hardly say nobody had warned them.

The following day, 21 August, as the rash of summer strikes spread to Felixstowe (the first for thirty years at the great container port), I put down a mood piece in my diary:

> There's a feeling of creeping paralysis – of nothing working – abroad in the country; a mixture of fatalism and resentment … [Earlier] … in the pages of this diary … I wrote of an 'autumn of discontent'. We're now slap bang in the middle of a 'summer of discontent' with the storm clouds of another 'autumn and winter of discontent' already gathering. Perhaps our political/social/economic vocabulary should change to the simplicity of a single word – DISCONTENT. Later we can decide whether it should be stretched to 'year' or 'age of discontent'.
>
> Thank heaven the sun is bright on the [Scapa] Flow and the fields shine green – great dispellers both of gathering gloom.
>
> In the meantime, there are but 2 weeks left for 150,000 of our people to determine whose set of prejudices best reflect theirs before deciding, on behalf of 66m of the rest of us, whose face and set of grey cells will turn on the cornucopia of problems that face us.

Just when you thought Truss's unfitness for the top job could not be more clearly demonstrated in terms of her weakness for insulting those with whom she would need to deal and, indeed, was dealing with as foreign secretary, this exchange occurred on the evening of Thursday 25 August at a hustings in Norwich moderated by Julia Hartley-Brewer:

HARTLEY-BREWER: President Macron. Friend or foe?
TRUSS: The jury is out.

This will long be remembered as a low point in the history of UK diplomacy, a craft at which we like to think we excel. 'The crassness of that reply,' I wrote,

> is hard to absorb. It is evidence of an emptiness of mind breath-taking in a UK Foreign Secretary. Does she not think before she speaks? If she did it makes it all the worse.
>
> We have collapsed as a diplomatic trading nation (as my old friend Geoffrey Smith used to put it). All those years since 1945 trying to shore up our influence in the world – the best efforts of all those PMs, Foreign Secretaries, Diplomats, Intelligence people – it comes down to one asinine moment in East Anglia. Her defenders say she said it with a chuckle; a kind of joke; her audience loved it. As if that explains it away; somehow makes it right.
>
> The conclusion? We are now PUNCHING LIGHTER THAN OUR WEIGHT. And to think, in just over a week's time, this lady will probably be the Queen's First Minister. How have we been brought so low?

I ended my lament by the Flow wondering: 'How will Macron respond?'

With care and dignity, was the answer. On a visit to Algeria, Macron said the UK was a friendly nation, sometimes despite its leaders. But he warned of possible 'serious problems' to come in the Anglo-French relationship if the British could not say if they were friends or enemies.

Alistair Burt, the respected former FO minister, described Truss's remark as a 'serious error'.[22] Gavin Barwell, Theresa May's chief of staff in No. 10, was tartly effective: 'You would have thought the Foreign Secretary was aware we are in a military alliance with

France.'[23] David Gauke, the former lord chancellor, captured whole the problem with the hustings: 'There's playing to the gallery and then there's letting the prejudices of the gallery go to your head.'[24]

The domestic scene darkened on Friday 26 August with the long-anticipated announcement from the Office of Gas and Electricity Markets (Ofgem) that the average energy cap for households would rise by 80 per cent on 1 October to £3,549. The indicators were that this would rise further to £5,000 next January and £6,000 by next April. Ofgem recognised that this would be 'devastating'.

I noted that:

> It won't hold; it can't hold. A really hefty shaft of government intervention will be needed to avert individual and collective catastrophes that would befall every street in the land unless the government moves. This is one of those crises whose ramifications and implications everyone understands and about which everybody subscribes to their own general theory of heating, lighting, and money. It is also one of those moments when the model of regulatory liberal capitalism is severely tested.

And two days later, on Sunday 28 August, I wrote:

> Two shafts of political wit lighten the political gloom.
> Before breakfast, my younger daughter, Polly, and I have a chat about the ghastliness of political life. Poll says she can't bear the irrationality of the extremes of left and right:
> 'I love the boring centre. They're my people,' she says.

In the early afternoon (when the newspapers arrive in South Ronaldsay), we found Andrew Rawnsley had this delicious line in his *Observer* column: 'Social services should step in and take Britain away from the Conservatives on the grounds of neglect.'

More importantly, Andrew shone a light on a truly worrying

black hole in the leadership debates – the lack of attention to the very factor that brought Johnson down:

> The contenders have … failed to say how they would restore integrity to our public life after the debaucheries of the Johnson premiership. This contest is happening because the outgoing prime minister was fired by his MPs for being unfit to hold the office he disgraced. Yet there has been no reckoning with his sleaze, rule-breaking and mendacities. Mr Sunak hasn't wanted to go there because many Tory members remain entranced by the Johnson cult and have fallen for the fiction that he was a colossus brought down by treacherous colleagues.
>
> Ms Truss has calculated that her ambitions are best served by presenting herself as loyal towards 'a fantastic prime minister' and propagating the myth that Mr Johnson was the victim of betrayal rather than the architect of his own downfall.
>
> Alarmingly for anyone who hoped that a change at Number 10 would usher in a more ethical regime, she has refused to commit to filling the position of standards invigilator left vacant since the last one quit in disgust with Mr Johnson. She has also voiced opposition to the parliamentary inquiry into whether the departing prime minister lied to the Commons about Partygate.[25]

The tocsins continued to ring out warnings about the placing of Truss's hands on the levers of economic policy. In an interview with *The Times* on 29 August, the hugely authoritative Paul Johnson of the Institute for Fiscal Studies accused Truss of pushing a 'simplistic mantra' on tax-cutting as a means of easing cost-of-living worries. Some of her possible policies were 'quite worrying', he said. If she went ahead with tens of billions' worth of tax cuts she would 'completely crash the public finances'.[26]

Liz Truss herself contributed further to this lack of confidence by pulling out of an interview with the BBC's Nick Robinson, as she had earlier from a session with Andrew Neil on Channel 4.

She wouldn't be able to blank out the markets if she became PM. They wouldn't need a television studio to expose her political incompetence.

On the sea-change question, could a Truss disaster engineer one of those huge cyclical events comparable to the discrediting of laissez-faire capitalism after the Great Crash of 1929 and the ensuing depression in the 1930s, which gave life to the 'never again' politico-economic impulse that contributed to Attlee's huge majority in 1945? This was the theme I pondered as we entered September 2022, in the knowledge that a Truss premiership was overwhelmingly likely in just a few days.

6

Operation London Bridge

Among my contemporaries, I am reckoned
to have weathered rather well.

Queen Elizabeth II in her mid-seventies[1]

Just occasionally in the life of a diarist, a single sentence retrospectively takes on immense significance.

FRIDAY 2 SEPTEMBER 2022
HMQ will miss tomorrow's Braemar Games.

Year in, year out, the occasion was one of pure delight for the Queen. Cabers were tossed, reels danced, kilts sported by the royal males, the finest tweeds worn by the sovereign. A crucial part of the refreshing of body and spirit during the Queen's summers at Balmoral. She would not miss the Braemar Games lightly. Something was up.

Away from the spectacle of sunlight on tartan, the dreary – but crucial – theme of political economy continued to make the political weather. Listen to the very well-connected James Forsyth in his Friday column for *The Times*:

If the new prime minister cannot solve the energy bills problem, then their premiership could be over before it has really begun. But while fuel bills are the biggest driver of public concern, there is a broader problem with dismal regulation of energy and water turning the public against privatisation, and against market economics more broadly.[2]

Truss could be the one who really did turn the terms of trade in the tussle between the 'isms' that gives British politics so much of its motive power.

At the start of September, such deep-swell questions in the tides of UK political economy were superseded by a truly alarming rumour.

SUNDAY 4 SEPTEMBER 2022
Much talk of a Johnson run to retake No.10 when, as he has been putting it to his friends, he has acquired sufficient 'hay in the loft' (i.e., money to pay off his debts plus more to fund his lifestyle). All this plus reports that he will try, with Truss's help, to thwart the H of C Privileges Committee on the misleading Parliament allegations mean that he is *pre*-haunting *post*-Johnson politics before his successor has been announced.

The following day, Liz Truss had her shining hour in the QEII Centre just across the road from Parliament:

MONDAY 5 SEPTEMBER 2022
12:15 Graham Brady
172,437 eligible to vote
82.6% turnout
RISHI SUNAK 60,399 (42.6%)
LIZ TRUSS   81,326 (57.4%)

Closer than expected.

Her husband, Hugh O'Leary, hands her her text and pats her arm. She does not kiss or touch him as she gets up from her chair before sweeping past Sunak, neither offering him her hand or even looking at him, on the way to the podium to deliver her short, rather staccato speech.

She is effusive in her praise of Johnson and his achievements.

'I campaigned as a Conservative. I shall govern as a Conservative' i.e., no early general election.

Liz Truss had demonstrated her one outstanding skill. She had taken the most cherished beliefs of the Conservative activists, polished them up, and given them back to them – all shiny and renewed – with an implicit message: the world may have changed, it may be distressingly baffling, but *your* prejudices still fit. Yours are the true insights. They represent what we most need. It reminded me of J. K. Galbraith's fascinating chapter on 'The Concept of the Conventional Wisdom' in his 1958 classic *The Affluent Society*, in which he wrote that 'the hallmark of the conventional wisdom is acceptability. It has the approval of those to whom it is addressed. There are many reasons why people like to hear articulated that which they approve. It serves the ego ... To hear what he believes is ... a source of reassurance.'[3] Not only do conventional wisdoms bring joy to activists of all kinds; we all relish them in varying degrees. They validate us. Crucially, they induce warm feelings towards those who play them back to us. But when confined to a particular tribal reservation of the political kind, they are a pain and – if they are the final determinant of who shall be our prime minister – inadequate at best and positively dangerous at worst: a consolation that can come at a very high price. And determinant they were – albeit for a few weeks – in September 2022.

On the day of Liz Truss's victory, 6 September 2022, I composed a 'reflection':

So begins a new age in our political geology ... the Trussian era. Will it be short-lived, laying down a meagre fossil trail? Will it take many (including me) by surprise by leaving a rich seam of achievement? Or, to change metaphors, have we witnessed today a large, upward step in the rise of the mediocracy in British political life? I fear so.

On *The World This Weekend* the previous day, the shrewd, always direct Patience Wheatcroft rightly told Jonny Dymond that Liz Truss faced 'the most intimidating in-tray ever'.

The next day, I made an attempt to imagine the in-tray that would await when she returned from seeing the Queen at Balmoral:

Energy, inflation, cost of living.
Russia/Ukraine.
Northern Ireland Protocol.
Brexit effects generally.
The ever-stubborn productivity problem.
Climate change and the COP26 targets.
The financing of health and social care.
Sustaining the Union of the UK.

How to revive a country suffused in the politics of pessimism in which nothing seems to work.

PLUS THE PERSONAL ONE

Of how to quickly broaden and deepen herself leaving behind an image of a narrow, meagre, partisan ideological individual who rates her capacities to such a degree that her pretension/ performance equation touches the delusory.

Prime ministerial transitions always carry a high electrical charge, whether it's the electorate that has done the ejecting or the ejected one's party – or even if they go willingly (as with Harold Wilson in 1976). This time, it was supercharged, for within two days of Johnson flying to Deeside to resign, as a country and as a kingdom, we were never the same again.

TUESDAY 6 SEPTEMBER 2022

7:30 a.m. Johnson leaves No.10 with a touch of bitterness claiming the '22 had changed the rules half-way (they hadn't though there was talk of it). He reprises his achievements (Brexit; vaccine; Ukraine).

'I'm now like one of those booster rockets that has fulfilled its function.'

He then alluded to Cincinnatus (who returned to his farm having saved Rome – and then came back again). Is all this a tease? I suspect it is not entirely. He is still inhaling his own legend.

He flies to Aberdeen, then up the Dee Valley to Balmoral, resigning about noon. Liz Truss arrives 10 minutes late in a Highland downpour.

12:20 p.m. HMQ asks her to form an administration in one of her private drawing rooms at Balmoral.

1:00 p.m. The new PM leaves Balmoral for Aberdeen airport.

As Liz Truss made her way back to London, there was a rush of reports on the likely scale of the new government's energy prices intervention. It could cost between £100 and £130 billion and would involve capping bills well into next year at a rate of £20–30 billion a quarter. Bills would be repaid over ten to twenty years. The energy companies meanwhile would have access to a government-backed fund. If these figures are anywhere near right, this would lose the Exchequer about a quarter of the cost of Covid.

At about 4:30 [p.m.], Downing Street fills up with Truss supporters. A fierce burst of rainfall sends them scurrying into No.9 … The podium is taken indoors. The commentariat's umbrellas go up; they fret about water getting into their electrics. The weather clears; the podium reappears.

At 5:06 [p.m.], LT arrives in Downing Street; walks from the Range Rover straight to the podium without working the crowd.

She starts with praise of Johnson.

She places 'freedom, enterprise, fair play' at the centre of her programmes so that 'we can become the modern, brilliant Britain'.

Without naming him, she paid homage to Winston Churchill: 'I will take action this day and every day.'

In homage to Baldrick (as Niddy pointed out), she pledged a 'bold plan' for economic growth and for tackling the energy crisis. 'We will transform Britain into an aspiration nation.'

'We shouldn't be daunted … We can ride out the storm.'

Liz Truss spoke for about four to five minutes before walking purposefully through the fabled door of great – and sometimes poignant – entries and exits. The clock started running from that very moment, as it does for every premiership, and her views and her personality began to impose themselves not just on the government machine but on the tone of our country and the face it presented to the world.

'With the very first spate of her appointments, it becomes plain that it will be a Cabinet above all of her people rather than an administration reflective of British Conservatism – a strategic decision in itself whose wisdom will be tested when troubles hit, which they will very shortly,' I wrote in my diary. As expected, the top beneficiaries were Kwasi Kwarteng to the Treasury, James Cleverly to the Foreign Office, and Suella Braverman to the Home Office, plus 'a Cabinet Room dominated by ideologues', as I wrote in my diary on 6 September.

In fact, trouble came fast. On the following morning, Wednesday 7 September, the pound fell to $1.14, its lowest rate against the US dollar since 1985. Kwasi Kwarteng was filmed in conversation with Andrew Bailey telling him that he (Kwarteng) would not be removing the Bank of England's independence. For its part, the Bank warned about the inflationary effect of tax cuts.

THURSDAY 8 SEPTEMBER 2022
THE DAY QUEEN ELIZABETH II DIED AT BALMORAL
The day we had dreaded and anticipated like no other.

John Major said: 'It's heart-breaking news … very hard to take in … The radiant smile that lights up a room and lights up the country.'

John is absolutely right.

A LIGHT GOES OUT

In the gloom of a wet Scottish afternoon in early September 2022, a very special light went out – a light which had dazzled a kingdom, a Commonwealth and a world for 70 years.

Its beam has shone through 15 premierships, albeit but two days for the final one; a social revolution or two; dramatic scientific and technological leaps; a 40-year Cold War lived in the shadow of the Bomb; a shedding of Empire and a morphing into a voluntary-association Commonwealth; an entry into a clustering European Community and an exit from an ever larger one. It was a beam remarkable for its steadiness and an ability to brighten up the lives of others.

In an instant what one might call 'The National Portrait' changed – the individual one we carry in our own heads; the collective picture we share and the canvas, with the Queen at its centre, we present as our portrait to the world. All these changed as a late summer rain fell on Deeside.

[As Justin Welby, the archbishop of Canterbury, put it on Friday's *Today* programme, when talking to her, 'You felt that history was in front of you.' That's certainly how I felt when it became plain the queen was dying.]

The notes for this diary entry that I was preparing this morning were about the new Prime Minister unveiling her government's energy emergency strategy. All that stopped at:

1:16 [p.m.] when Andy Marr rings to tell me the Queen is dying.

1:20 [p.m.] The BBC reports that members of the Royal Family are on their way to Balmoral, that the Queen is under medical supervision and that the doctors are concerned about her condition.* Robert Hardman says: 'She is where she is happiest.'

1:45 [p.m.] Reported that Prince Charles and the Princess Royal have arrived at Balmoral.

1:52 [p.m.] Huw Edwards takes over BBC rolling news. I scribble 'OPERATION LONDON BRIDGE IS STARTING' [The long-planned and regularly exercised contingency plan for the Queen's death and all that will happen from that moment until she is interred in the family vault in St George's Chapel, Windsor].

2:00 [p.m.] Another old journalist friend rings. He has heard from a member of the Privy Council that she may be dead already.

2:30 [p.m.] Another figure at the heart of a big news gathering operation tells me: 'They sounded the warning bell this morning and an announcement is expected this afternoon.'
    Feelings of deepening sadness and a kind of emptiness.
    If it happens it will be the sharpest *loss* for a country in *peril* – the sharpness all the greater because of the general and widespread anxiety.

4:30 [p.m.] Hear later that Simon C [Case] informs the PM of the Queen's death.

6:00 [p.m.] All her children are now at Balmoral.

---

* I discovered afterwards that Buckingham Palace released the original bulletin at 12:20 p.m. From the death certificate we learned later that the Queen had died at 3:10 p.m. The cause? 'Old age'.

6:30 [p.m.] Buckingham Palace announce that the 'Queen died peacefully at Balmoral this afternoon. The King and the Queen Consort will stay at Balmoral overnight and travel to London tomorrow.'

Huw Edwards is much moved reading the bulletin.

A rainbow appears in the sky above the lowered flag atop the great tower at Windsor Castle.

President Macron says: 'I remember her as a *friend* of France.'

7:00 [p.m.] The King releases his statement: 'The death of my beloved Mother, Her Majesty The Queen, is a moment of the greatest sadness for me and all members of my family. We mourn profoundly the passing of a cherished Sovereign and a much-loved mother. I know her loss will be deeply felt throughout the country, the Realms and the Commonwealth, and by countless people around the world. During this period of mourning and change, my family and I will be comforted and sustained by our knowledge of the respect and deep affection in which The Queen was so widely held.'[4]

7:07 [p.m.] The PM steps out of No.10 and up to the podium in Downing Street: 'We are all devastated … Queen Elizabeth is the rock on which modern Britain was built … She was the very spirit of Great Britain.' She referred to King Charles III (the first confirmation of his Kingly name). 'God Save The King.'

Nicola Sturgeon described it as 'a profoundly sad moment'.

Keir Starmer stressed her devotion to public service and how she 'stood not for what the nation fought over but what it agreed upon'.

David Cameron described her as: 'The world's greatest public servant and its most experienced diplomat.'

It was almost too much to absorb.

FRIDAY 9 SEPTEMBER 2022

RMT and Communications workers suspend planned strikes.

Commons and Lords tributes to HMQ.

PM going to see the King at 4:00 [p.m.]

The King's speech is very fine and very moving, crafted to carry a great deal of freight and much feeling. He delivered it from BP at 6:00 [p.m.] It struck me as his covenant with his people. The passages on the Constitution (respect for) were striking. I suspect their significance went beyond HMK signalling that he understood the limitations of a constitutional monarchy but also his sensitivity to the need to sustain the historical conventions …

> In that faith [the Church of England], and the values it inspires,
> I have been brought up to cherish a sense of duty to others,
> and to hold in the greatest respect the precious traditions,
> freedoms, and responsibilities of our unique history and our
> system of parliamentary government.
> As The Queen herself did with such unswerving devotion,
> I too now solemnly pledge myself throughout the remaining
> time God grants me to uphold the constitutional principles at
> the heart of our nation.[5]

As I watched him deliver it on the television, I underlined the constitutional principles at the heart of our nation … The microphones did their historical work.

To the crowd outside BP, he said: 'I've been dreading it.' He said the same to the PM when he welcomed her to their first audience … He [also] said: 'We mustn't take up too much of your time.'

Of all the foreign leaders who sent condolences, Macron was rather wonderful:

'To you, she is your Queen. To us, she is *The* Queen. To us all, she will be with us forever.'

SATURDAY 10 SEPTEMBER 2022
10:00 [a.m.] ST JAMES'S PALACE
THE PROCLAMATION OF HIS MAJESTY THE KING

200 Privy counsellors gather in the Picture Gallery. All the surviving prime ministers are there; the Archbishops; the 2 Speakers [Lindsay Hoyle and John McFall]; Sturgeon and Salmond; former party leaders such as Neil Kinnock and Michael Howard.

The PCs are asked to turn-off their mobiles.

The Lord President, Penny Mordaunt, proposes that a deputation shall wait upon the King in the Throne Room.

Richard Tilbrook, Clerk of the Privy Council, reads out the 'Proclamation'.

All cry 'GOD SAVE THE KING!'

The platform party sign the Proclamation.

There is a pin-drop silence.

The King reads his Declaration in a firm voice.

Once again, he pledges to uphold constitutional government:

I am deeply aware of this great inheritance and of the duties and heavy responsibilities of Sovereignty which have now passed to me. In taking up these responsibilities, I shall strive to follow the inspiring example I have been set in upholding constitutional government and to seek the peace, harmony and prosperity of the people of these Islands and of the Commonwealth Realms and Territories throughout the world.[6]

The sound of the military bands striking up drifts in.

To the side, standing together, are Clive Alderton, Edward Young [joint private secretaries to the king] and Simon Case.

10:39 [a.m.] The Council's business ends.

10:56 [a.m.] State trumpeters sound. The Proclamation Party

appears on the balcony (Garter King of Arms, The Earl Marshal, the Serjeant at Arms).

11:00 [a.m.] Great blast of top-flight trumpeting. Garter reads [The Proclamation]

The Coldstream [Guards] present Arms.

GOD SAVE THE KING!

Another great blast on the trumpets … Garter calls for three cheers.

11:05 [a.m.] Platform Party go back in.

Gun salutes at the Tower, in Hyde Park, and in Edinburgh Castle.

In Windsor, the Cambridges and the Sussexes work the crowd together quite unexpectedly.

At BP in the afternoon HMK receives the PM and Cabinet and the opposition parties.

Truss will accompany the King as he travels around his Kingdom during the coming week.

SUNDAY 11 SEPTEMBER 2022
HMQ travels by hearse from Balmoral to Edinburgh Proclamations in Edinburgh, Cardiff, and Belfast.

Poll [my daughter] has a nice line of HMQ: 'She was constant. She just turned up whenever she was needed.'

MONDAY 12 SEPTEMBER 2022
10:35 [a.m.] The King addresses both Houses of Parliament in Westminster Hall where he told them: 'I cannot help but feel the weight of history which reminds us of the vital Parliamentary traditions to which members of both houses dedicate yourselves with such personal commitment for the betterment of us all.'

Then there it was again, the ringing paean of praise to

'precious' constitutional principles: 'While very young, Her late Majesty pledged herself to serve her country and her people and to maintain the precious principles of constitutional government which lie at the heart of our nation. This vow she kept with unsurpassed devotion.'[7]

Then off to Edinburgh for Holyrood, St. Giles, and the Parliament where he spoke of 'that deep and abiding bond' between HMQ and Scotland.

TUESDAY 13 SEPTEMBER 2022.
HMK flies to Belfast. Alex Maskey (Sinn Fein), Presiding Officer, NI Assembly, reads condolence. HM replies.

As he signs the visitors' book at Hillsborough, his pen gives out. 'Every stinking time,' he says as Camilla rushes to his aid and his flash of irritation is beamed round the world (he must be exhausted). Then into central Belfast.

HMQ leaves Scotland for the last time in an RAF Voyager lifting her high from Edinburgh Airport accompanied by the Princess Royal. Some 33,000 people had filed past her coffin in St. Giles before it was taken from the cathedral as a lone piper played 'The Flower of the Forest'. The Princess Royal says how privileged she was to have shared the last 24 hours of her mother's life [with her].

Huge crowds all the way from RAF Northolt to BP.

Like so many others, I still haven't absorbed her passing.

WEDNESDAY 14 SEPTEMBER 2022
BP TO WESTMINSTER HALL
At about 3:50 [p.m.] the bands strike up Beethoven's Funeral March and HMQ's coffin atop its gun carriage emerges escorted by her family. Down a packed Mall past the statues of her mother and father up the steps to Carlton Terrace Gardens (will she join them in due course?) Through Horse Guards. Down Whitehall. 38 minutes in all beneath bright, late-summer sunshine.

Big Ben tolled every minute. On that minute, the Royal Artillery fired in Hyde Park.

In Westminster Hall, Justin Welby leads the service.

As Nicholas Soames said later on *Channel 4 News*: 'The Royal Family hands the Queen back to the nation.'

A 3-mile queue of respect-payers builds up along the South Bank of the River Thames.

THURSDAY 15 SEPTEMBER 2022

The queue for Westminster Hall is now 4 ½ miles long; the wait is 8 hours [it reaches 24 hours in the evening].

On *Channel 4 News*, Justin Welby says the Queen practiced 'servant leadership'.

Paddy O'Connell is coming to Walthamstow to record a piece for Sunday's 'Broadcasting House', on the eve of the Queen's internment at Windsor. I prepare a few notes and thoughts that I have been scribbling in bits over the past few days:

THE SANDRINGHAM CRITERIA

She remained the fixture as, all around her, the fittings changed.

So far, the Queen's Sandringham wish has been fulfilled. It suffused everything King Charles has said. In those few sentences, she described the values that had been the lodestar of her life, and, at the same time, held them up to guide not just her successor but everyone engaged in the national conversation, indeed, beyond. 'I commend them to everyone,' she said. I thought it was quietly powerful at the time she spoke at the Sandringham WI. It remains so – very much so – as we ponder the kingdom to come.

HOW TO PAINT A PORTRAIT OF THE QUEEN? THE QUEEN AS A NATIONAL PORTRAIT GALLERY IN HER OWN PERSON

1: An individual one in the sense of the picture we accumulated of her in our own heads – as a presence, rather like our families, throughout our conscious lives.

2: A national one. The impeccable bearer of public duties who, in constitutional matters, never put a foot wrong. Part, too, of the emotional geography of our national life – there at the moments of sadness and anxiety as well as of joy and celebration.

3: Crucial to the portrait we as a country display to the world – the most dazzling instrument of 'soft power' we (or any other country, come to that) have ever possessed. She carried in her person the kind of power that armies, fleets, and squadrons cannot.

The link between all three parts of the Elizabethan Portrait Gallery? What Martin Charteris called her 'tonic quality'. She was our number one life-enhancer – a wonderful quality to possess. It was one of the key reasons that she brought the best out of people on, as the decades passed, an increasingly heroic scale.

FRIDAY 16 SEPTEMBER 2022
The King is in Cardiff. Receives the condolences of the Senedd. Then to a service in Llandaff Cathedral. Excellent harping. 'Cwm Rhondda'. 'I vow to Thee My Country'.

Reception at Cardiff Castle. HMK tells Mark Drakeford about his concerns over the rising cost of living.

Returns to London and a meeting of faith leaders in BP, he talks of his 'duty to protect the diversity of our country'.

As world leaders arrive, the Met Police say they are mounting their biggest ever operation.

Robin Janvrin [the Queen's private secretary, 1999–2007] says it's 'extraordinarily humbling. It's been so beautifully organised … the contact between us, the people, and our departed Queen. [Monday] will be a real moment of national catharsis.'

At 7:30 [p.m.], the Queen's four children mount her guard of honour.

Over the weekend, I'm sent a copy of William Waldegrave's beautifully crafted tribute to the Queen delivered in Eton College Chapel (where William is Provost) on 11 September. He asks:

What is it that is happening to us and to many, many millions of people not just here in the United Kingdom, but around the world, which make this old lady's death leave us feeling so profoundly moved and so bereft? Why is it that we feel such genuine and heartfelt grief?

It is not that the old lady was some titanic writer or scientist, some politician or soldier who had led nations to triumph or glory, some Mandela or Tolstoy or Newton or Napoleon. Not at all. She was an honest, decent, hardworking woman with a sharp sense of humour and a heavenly smile; an iron memory for faces, a fascination with people, a great expertise in blood-stock, an affection for this place which she often visited, and a quiet but profound Christian faith, the rock on which she built her life.

William concluded by talking of 'the values of service, self-effacement and duty, often so under-rated in the rat races for power, money or fame which surrounds us' and stressed that the 'quietly heroic old lady represented to us and for us all that is best in us.'

These paragraphs, the finest piece of encapsulated biography I have ever read, will not be bettered when historians come to sift the tributes to her seventy years headship of state and her conduct of monarchy at the heart of what my friend, the writer Ellie Updale, described to me as 'the fragile crystal ball of the constitution'.

At 8 p.m. on Sunday 18 September there was a two-minute national silence.

MONDAY 19 SEPTEMBER 2022
THE FUNERAL OF QUEEN ELIZABETH II
THE END OF THE POSTWAR ERA

10:40 [a.m.] Absolute stillness in Palace Yard as the gun carriage and 142 naval ratings await the coffin.

10:42 [a.m.] The Grenadier Guards carry out the coffin followed by the King (in naval uniform) and the Royal Family.

10:46 [a.m.] The pipes and drums (instant bringers of emotion) strike up their potent aural blend and the slow march to Westminster Abbey begins where 2000 people (500 of them foreign leaders and dignitaries) wait. The Abbey's bell tolls.

10:54 [a.m.] The procession halts before the Great West Door of the Abbey.

10:58 [a.m.] The coffin enters the Abbey.

11:05 a.m. The guardsmen place the coffin on the catafalque.

11:07 [a.m.] The Dean begins the service ... 'a place where remembrance and hope are sacred duties ... an unswerving commitment to a high calling ... her life-long sense of duty'.

'The day thou gavest, Lord is ending ...'

11:15 [a.m.] Patricia Scotland [secretary general of the Commonwealth] reads a lesson. 'Oh Death, where is thy sting ...'

11:22 [a.m.] Liz Truss reads a lesson. 'In my Father's House there are many mansions ...'

11:27 [a.m.] Justin Welby's sermon. It had beauty; it had bite.

'People of loving service are rare in any walk of life. Leaders of long service are still rarer. But in all cases those who serve will be loved and remembered when those who cling to power and privileges are long forgotten.'

'My soul, there is a country' (Hubert Parry)

PRAYERS (faith leaders)

'O Taste and See' (Ralph Vaughn Williams)

LORD'S PRAYER

'Love Divine'

ARCHBISHOP OF CANTERBURY PRAYERS 'Go forth, O Christian soul'.

'Who shall separate us?' (James Macmillan)

11:55 [a.m.] Dean's blessing.

STATE TRUMPETERS

THE SILENCE

THE BLESSING

TRUMPETERS

THE LAST POST

12:00 [p.m.] THE NATIONAL ANTHEM

12:02 [p.m.] THE LONE PIPER (in a gallery)

The Queen's Piper (Pipe Major Paul Burns)

'Sleep, dearie, sleep'

12:07 [p.m.] Grenadier bearers place the coffin on their shoulders.

12:15 [p.m.] Coffin leaves through the Great West Door and into the sunshine.

12:30 [p.m.] Procession moves off led by 4 Mounties dazzling in scarlet. The Massed Bands strike up Beethoven's Funeral March. The Abbey Bell tolls. The coffin passes the Cenotaph.*

12:38 [p.m.] The gun carriage passes through Horse Guards Arch.

12:55 [p.m.] Half-way down The Mall, the bands change to 'The Dead March' from 'Saul'.

1:05 [p.m.] The Queen approaches Buckingham Palace for the last time. Her staff line the pavement.

1:07 [p.m.] She passes BP's Main Gate.

1:20 [p.m.] Procession approaches the Wellington Arch. Guns fire in Hyde Park, Naval pipers sound as coffin transferred by the Grenadiers from the gun carriage into the hearse. It's silent and still now.

1:37 [p.m.] Hearse moves off to the sound of the National Anthem.

* The juxtaposition was too much for me and I started to weep.

Applause and flowers from the crowd as the cortege heads west towards Knightsbridge.

Huge crowds line the Long Walk leading up to Windsor Castle. In a lovely touch, her last pony stands with a groom; also on display one of HMQ's riding headscarves.

3:50 [p.m.] Procession passes through the gate into the castle's Quadrangle, the hearse still strewn with flowers.

3:55 [p.m.] Through the George IV Arch her family and two corgis await her.

3:59 [p.m.] The piper's play 'The Flowers of the Forest'.

4:07 [p.m.] The bell tolls. The Grenadiers carry HMQ up the steps.
    The choir sings Psalm 121. 'I raise mine eyes unto the hills…'
    They sing the Russian 'Kontakion of the Departed' as they did at Prince Philip's funeral.

4:24 [p.m.] The Dean of Windsor reads The Bidding. 'Kindness and concern … her calm and dignified presence has given us confidence to face the future with courage and hope.'
    'All My Hope on God is Founded …'
    A reading from the Book of Revelation: 'I saw a new Heaven and a new Earth … a new Jerusalem … For the former things are passed away. It is done. I am Alpha and Omega, the beginning and the end.'
    Prayers from the Vicar of Sandringham, the Minister of Crathie and the Chaplain of the Royal Chapel.

THE LORDS PRAYER

4:38 [p.m.] The Instruments of State are removed from the coffin. The Orb, the Sceptre and the Imperial State Crown are given to the Dean of Windsor who lays them on cushions placed on top of the altar.

'Christ is made the Sure Foundation' (Henry Purcell)

4:45 [p.m.] The Lord Chamberlain, Andrew Parker, breaks his wand of office into two; both parts will be interred with HMQ.

As the coffin begins to sink slowly into the vault, the Dean of Windsor says: 'Go forth from this world, O Christian Soul.'

4:50 [p.m.] The Lone Piper plays and fades away into the distance.

The Archbishop says: 'Go forth into the world in peace.'

THE BLESSING

The coffin lowers into the vault.

THE NATIONAL ANTHEM

4:54 [p.m.] The Royal Family leave the chapel to the sound of J. S. Bach's 'Prelude and Fugue'.

On the way out the King has a word with the Archbishop.

At about 7:30 [p.m.], at a private family service, Elizabeth II is laid to rest in the vault with her father, mother and husband and the ashes of her sister Margaret.

THE POSTWAR ERA ENDS

The kingdom is already different. The scenery and the lighting have changed. The emotional geography will never be the same again. Nor will the arc on which we travel singly or together. She paved it with gold. She was *the* gold-standard constitutional monarch.

Was There an Elizabethan Era?

The vast majority of her subjects had never known a time when
Queen Victoria had not been reigning over them. She had
become an indissoluble part of their whole scheme of things.

Lytton Strachey on 20 January 1901 (the day the public
were told of Queen Victoria's imminent death)[1]

So as our great Elizabethan era comes to an end, we
will honour the late Queen's memory by keeping alive
the values of public service she embodied.

Sir Keir Starmer, 8 September 2022[2]

For all the differences in their character and in the country and
world in which they lived and breathed, what Strachey wrote of
Queen Victoria was true, too, of Queen Elizabeth II. It was on
Christmas Day 2018 that I sat down and began to think about the
question of an eponymous Elizabethan Age. Here are my 'Thoughts
on Christmas Day 2018' and the paragraphs I added over New Year
and into early January 2019:

I'm writing this a couple of hours before the Queen's Christmas
Broadcast to her country and her Commonwealth in an empty
house on South Ronaldsay in the Orkney Islands. Very soon
it will fill with noise, jollity and chat as the family return from
'The Boys' Ba', the rule-free ballgame which the men and boys
of Kirkwall play between 'The Doonies' and 'The Uppies' on

Christmas and New Years' Day and which is widely thought
to be the ancient and primitive original of football (two of my
grandsons, Joe and Jack Cromby, were on the losing 'Doonie'
side this morning after a fierce near-2 ½ hour tussle through the
streets of Kirkwall.[3]

The Queen's Broadcast was especially keenly anticipated
this year, not least by me. Would she choreograph one of her
'soft power disguised as hard power' moments (as one of her
former private secretaries likes to call them)[4] given the chaos and
uncertainty about Britain and Europe and her kingdom's place in
the world? Would there by a touch of 'pull yourself together' (as
another ex-member of her staff put it)[5] in her carefully crafted
words? The speech is hers; prepared with the help of her Palace
officials. It is not written on the advice of her ministers, though an
advance copy goes to No. 10 Downing Street as a courtesy.

By the time her message was broadcast we knew the answer. It
was yes.

Blazoned across yesterday's newspapers was her quiet hymn to
the pursuit of harmony amid discord. *The Daily Telegraph* splashed
its front page with a large photo of the Queen in mid-full flow of
recording her words under the headline and strapline:

Queen: UK must overcome 'deeply held differences'

Respect each other as human beings, she says in Christmas
address before Brexit.[6]

The key paragraph formed part of a passage on the
Commonwealth but its Brexit import was unmistakable. It
would have been the product of much thought – and careful
judgment – and the critical words had been put out in advance by
Buckingham Palace for the Christmas Eve newspapers (none are
published on Christmas Day).

'Even with the most deeply held differences, treating the other person with respect and as a fellow human being is always a good first step towards greater understanding.'

Adding a degree of poignancy for at least some of her listeners and viewers on Christmas afternoon was the unspoken fear that if the country lost its 92-year-old monarch in the midst of its grade-one listed Brexit political crisis it would be a psychological blow of very considerable magnitude – (a thought offered, interestingly, by a lady ambassador from a Communist country [Cuba, in fact] to a friend of mine at a City dinner a few weeks earlier).[7]

The European Question had been *the* great political disruptor of the Queen's reign – far more vexing and stretching than the other great geopolitical shift on her watch – the disposal of Britain's overseas territorial possessions and the shift from Empire to Commonwealth, an accomplishment to which she was absolutely central.

In the December days of 2018, as she prepared to record her broadcast to her country and her Commonwealth at Buckingham Palace on the 12th (the day after what was to have been the 'meaningful vote' on Mrs Theresa May's Brexit deal) and the Cabinet and the House of Commons struggled to find a way out of the Brexit paralysis, in my darker moments, watching events (or non-events) unfold from Westminster, I reckoned the only moving part of the British constitution that was constantly performing as the nation would wish it to was its monarchy. The political class, even the parliamentary system itself, seemed very far from coping with the paramount question of the day. We, her subjects, could sing 'God save the Queen'; she, even if she wished to, could not hum 'God save the country'. Her Christmas Day broadcast was the nearest she could get to it. As she gently put it to her 6.3 million viewers on BBC One and ITV (one in ten of the UK population):[8] 'Some cultures believe a long life brings wisdom. I'd like to think so.' In the Queen's case, we know so.

What I did not anticipate over the Christmas and New Year

period of 2018–19 was that within a month she would return to this theme in her Sandringham WI centenary address on Thursday 24 January 2019, with which I began this book. As the Brexit cacophony acquired still more decibels, the Queen struck a note of calm among the clamour while, in a way, painting a portrait of her country as she had perhaps imagined it in the past and always wished it to be.

Perhaps the most striking characteristic of the Queen's seventy-year reign was how she reconciled the timeless and the new in her country from the time of her accession on 6 February 1952; how she adjusted to its morphologies and deployed her duty of care for its well-being and its cohesion. A symbol of continuity at home and permanently of the highest star quality abroad. Though she was the subject of intense and unbroken media coverage for nearly ten decades, there nonetheless remained something elusive about Queen Elizabeth II, a shyness at the heart of her gift for putting people at their ease. After the dazzle of her early years as a beautiful young woman on the throne, the idea of a 'new Elizabethan era' largely lost its vitality. However, on Christmas Day in 2018 I came to the conclusion that the years of her reign had turned out to be exactly that.

Epochs, even the most obvious, are always difficult to define. Some find such delineations easier than others. Churchills are good at epochs. It was Sir Winston Churchill's grandson, Sir Nicholas Soames, who declared one morning as we arrived for work at Westminster during the prolonged post-Brexit referendum arguments: 'It's the end of the post-war settlement.' Elizabeth II was the queen of the post-war settlement – that is the 'big picture' of her reign, to borrow that metaphor she used at the Sandringham WI.

She was a young woman during the years of the Second World War that distilled the political fuel for that settlement and stimulated its blueprints for economic, health, and welfare reforms. She was an ever-conscientious heir-in-waiting to her father when the bigger of those blueprints were turned into institutions and social programmes in the first years of peace. She became monarch at the high-water mark of consensus between the political parties (a condition she profoundly wished for her people and her kingdom).

Elizabeth II was also the queen of the age of adjustment. She was crucial to the shift from territorial empire to free-association Commonwealth. She saw out the great forty-year confrontation of the Cold War. Her reign was almost coterminous with the Britain-and-Europe question in its modern form. She carefully observed a social revolution in terms of the values, the living standards, indeed the very make-up of the population of these islands. She was the fixture when the fittings seemed to change – some, not all, because there were multiple continuities for whose importance she possessed a special feel. Her life, her duties and her example ran through those years like a seam of superglue.

The monarchy under Elizabeth II's stewardship was never in the vanguard of change nor an exercise in conscious modernity, but it was sensitive to the pacemakers both at home and abroad. Yet her personality and her style were consistencies among the rush of events and never so important than at times of anxiety such as the Covid years and during the political turbulence which disturbed the last year of her reign.

It is this consistency and continuity that lies at the heart of the claim that there *was* an Elizabethan age coterminous with the post-war era – though in a very different way from Victoria's let alone from that of Elizabeth I. Her very longevity, naturally, made her what Sir David Manning, former ambassador to Washington, called 'living history'.[9] But there was much more to her era than that.

Elizabeth II was the symbol – perhaps the incarnation – of continuity within her kingdom (which was also part of her international appeal). There were continuities aplenty. Here are the key ones that span her reign:

- Perpetual worries about the relative performance of the British economy, the levels of productivity reached in its output of goods and services, its attempts to industrialise its science and technology and to cope with pressures in its economy and its balances of payments.

- Associated with this throughout the Queen's reign was the question of education, its structures and institutions – particularly the vitality of its technical elements. This was related to a wider continuity of anxieties about the divisive effects of social class and status among her subjects.

- A preoccupation with Britain's place in the world – how to cut a dash internationally greater than our resources would of themselves permit – popularised by one of her foreign secretaries, Douglas Hurd, as the punching-above-their-weight question.[10] The matter of Britain and Europe remained a crucial part of this throughout and a destabilising, often disruptive one.

- The UK became a nuclear weapons state seven months into her reign and has remained one ever since.

- The Union of the UK has remained intact, notwithstanding substantial devolution to Scotland, Wales, and Northern Ireland since the late 1990s, and the considerable stress that was placed upon it during the last years of her reign.

- The country still relies on a largely unwritten 'historic' constitution for its governing rules-of-the-game resting on precedent, convention, and procedure as well as laws – though much more of it came to be written down either in statute or in codes from the 1990s. Parts of the constitution came under considerable stress in the Johnson years.[11]

- The structure of political parties operated on a standard left-to-right model based on a first-past-the-post system for general elections fought as a tussle between liberal capitalism and social democracy. This model was under palpable strain during the last years of her reign largely, though not wholly, because of the Brexit question.

At the other end of the scale, what were the big shifts of the Eliza-bethan age?

- Empire into Commonwealth. She presided over more imperial disposals than her father (though the ending of empire in India was hugely significant, was dreadfully bloodstained, and involved enormous populations).
- The great European experiment, which began with the first application for membership of the EEC in July 1961, and ended with the formal departure from the EU and its treaties on 31 January 2020.
- The conduct and, above all, the ending of the Cold War after nearly forty years of her reign.
- The successive waves of globalisation that followed.
- Her era was almost coterminous with the computer age (the first commercial one was sold in the UK in 1951). But it was the last three decades of her reign that saw the widening of IT to everyday use by everyone and dramatic new dispositions of corporate and technical power, as well as dramatic changes in the print and electronic media.
- A huge shift from manufacturing to services in her kingdom's economy.
- A profound rearrangement in the makeup of the society over which she presided, with a dramatic shrinkage of the manual working class.
- Substantial population growth (from 46 million in 1952 to 66 million in 2021) and considerable changes in the ethnicities of that population.
- A surge in gender and sexual equalities alongside successive shifts in social attitudes and a weakening of deference all round.
- The rise of domestic terrorism, first relating to the resurgence of the troubles in Northern Ireland, later arising from the politics of jihadism.

- The coming and spreading of motorways.
- The replacement of steam by diesel and electricity on the railways.
- The revolution in airline travel.
- Successive transformations in drugs, treatments, and medical procedures.

We can be sure that Elizabeth II observed these changes with greater, more sustained and detailed attention than did Victoria observe the dramatic mutations of her kingdom between 1837 and 1901. From February 1952 the dutiful lady in Buckingham Palace watched all this carefully from her end of The Mall, as the endless succession of despatch riders and vans brought acres of official paper for her to read from the Whitehall ministries at the other end, and the diplomatic telegrams and intelligence reports kept her continually primed on what was going on abroad from her embassies and listening posts across the world.

Abroad she was an imperial Queen for nearly a decade, a European one for nearly five. At home she was the Queen of the post-war settlement as it played out after the essentials of the British New Deal had been put in place in the mid-to-late 1940s. It went through many refinements and alterations, but she reigned under the banner embroidered in those years. For me, that settlement went with her on her last journey to Windsor and her resting place in St George's Chapel. Future historians may well conclude that post-war Britain ended on that very day, when its constitutional monarch of seventy years was laid to rest, and with her, her extraordinary era.

There May Be Trouble Ahead

Governments can do dreadful things in their first heady months of office. I wish there could be a law against a new Government doing anything during its first three or so months of existence.

Lord Rothschild, former head of the central policy review staff, 1977[1]

There may be trouble ahead.

Irving Berlin, 'Let's Face the Music and Dance'[2]

There was. While we watched Operation London Bridge unfold, there were harbingers of how Liz Truss – a classic example of a prime minister in a hurry – would use the power and authority bestowed upon her by Queen Elizabeth's very last public duty in the private drawing room at Balmoral.

The public's attention, understandably, was very much elsewhere. But here were the signs of a *grade-one-listed* crisis to come – and soon, very soon – as the nation mourned. For those in the dealing rooms, where international money markets go about their cold, unsentimental business, their screens firmly fixed on the economic and political indicators rather than the queue for the catafalque along the South Bank, were nervy. The money people – including those who curated the great piles of mortgage investments and pension funds – did not like what they saw. Very swiftly they decided they did not rate the Truss–Kwarteng combination in No. 10 and No. 11 Downing Street and they began to move against them.

I lack such a city-trader screen, you will not be surprised to hear. But I caught some fragments on the filter of my daily diary:

WEDNESDAY 7 SEPTEMBER 2022
The Bank [of England] warns about the inflationary effect of tax cuts.

[At Prime Minister's Questions] Starmer talks of 'the fantasy of trickle-down economics'.

THURSDAY 8 SEPTEMBER 2022
Sterling at $1.15.

FRIDAY 9 SEPTEMBER 2022
Bill Keegan [veteran economics commentator of *The Observer*] comes to see us. Tells me Kwasi Kwarteng has sacked Tom Scholar [highly respected permanent secretary to the Treasury]. *Bad* news for the N-T [Northcote-Trevelyan] civil service.* Politicisation hovers, I fear.

WEDNESDAY 14 SEPTEMBER 2022
Becoming more worried about the partial, creeping politicisation of the senior civil service by the new PM. Part of the reason for Kwasi K firing Tom Scholar last week is that Liz Truss doesn't like him (private source). They didn't get on when she was Chief Secretary [to the Treasury].

Two days ago, Steven Swinford had the story in *The Times* that she had changed her plan to sack Simon Case. Apparently S impressed her with his transition preparations for her and her new government and with his handling of the Queen's death and after.[3]

* The model for the UK's non-political Civil Service was laid out in the Northcote-Trevelyan Report in 1853.

THURSDAY 15 SEPTEMBER 2022
Kwasi K's 'mini budget' will be delivered next Friday.

FRIDAY 16 SEPTEMBER 2022
The pound falls to a 37-year low against the dollar ($1.135) after worse than expected retail figures.

TUESDAY 20 SEPTEMBER 2022
Pound/dollar stands at $1.14.
Kwarteng refuses to publish Treasury forecast.

THURSDAY 22 SEPTEMBER 2022
Bank of England raises interest rates by 0.5% to 2.25%, the 7th consecutive rise. The Bank believes the economy may already be in recession. The IFS warns that government debt is being pushed up to 'an unsustainable level'. £1 = $1.13.

FRIDAY 23 SEPTEMBER 2022
Kwasi Kwarteng's mini budget that dare not speak its name.
'A new approach for a new era.'
Herewith the key elements Kwarteng described as 'central to solving the riddle of growth'.

- Scrapping of the 45% top rate of income tax for those earning £150,000 plus. They will pay 40%. A 1p in the pound cut to the basic rate will be brought forward to 2023.
- A 1.25% increase in national insurance contributions will be cut from November.
- Planned rise in corporation tax from 19% to 25% next April abandoned, putting £19bn a year into the economy.
- Cap on bankers' bonuses scrapped.
- Energy bills for households capped at an average of £2,500 a year for two years.

> Pound falls by 3.5% to $1.10 by midday after the announcements. Later it falls to $1.09 (the lowest since 1985). The markets don't like this.

In retrospect, this was the moment Liz Truss and Kwasi Kwarteng lost control personally, politically, economically. They never regained it. I wrote a more immediate assessment in my diary:

REFLECTION ON THE WEEK
The bands fell silent. The guards of honour returned to their barracks. World leaders stepped on to their planes home. The Queen was at rest in the family vault inside St. George's Chapel, Windsor.

Briefly there was silence – a silence swiftly broken by the whiny voice and the dreary prejudices of Britain's new Prime Minister. Then this morning Kwasi Kwarteng outlined the latest 'dash for growth', as it was called in 1962–3 when Harold Macmillan and Reggie Maudling tried to do the same.

Uplifting it was not. We were back in the depressing world of business-as-usual after a brief glimpse of our better selves. There was no sign of her or her ministers heeding the 'common ground' message that was central to the late Queen's words to the Sandringham WI. There is a consensus about the need for growth – but the tone and pitch of the Truss government is very far from consensual. And she still shows not the slightest sign of being able to reach those of our people outside the constricted ring and the narrow gauge of her and her Cabinet's ideology.

She utterly lacks a mind and a vocabulary that travels let alone moves and inspires. She has no feel for fairness – an impulse that always plays powerfully among the British people. They won't take to this. They won't take to her. And there's a strong possibility that the policies won't take either. For the Conservatives, it's a self-inflicted Black Wednesday – and worse. If the markets and the people are both unimpressed – that is a formidable combination.

We are better than this. We can do better than this. We *must* do better than this. The Truss–Kwarteng model of political economy is gambling the 2020s – not just its finances but its already precarious social peace. It does no honour to the Lady in the Vault. It does not help the new King. It brings naught for the comfort of his people. Its powerful pulse of deliberately generated inequality will tear at the fabric of the kingdom.

As for the period covered by this book (September 2021 to September 2022), it was a disturbed twelve months punctuated by upheaval, tawdry behaviour, and loss. There was, without doubt, still more trouble ahead.

The post-war era had ended, but not in a way any of the Queen's – and now the King's – subjects would have wished. She had left us her Sandringham WI criteria – her manifesto for beyond her reign. We had a great deal to live up to. The questions were *how* to and *could* we?

Notes

Preface: Standards High and Low

1 Quoted in Sam Coates, Katie Gibbons, Oliver Wright, 'Queen calls for end to Brexit feud', *The Times* (25 January 2019).
2 Queen Elizabeth II, *BBC1* (BBC Video, V 4710, 1992).
3 Oscar Wilde, 'The Importance of Being Earnest', in Timothy Gaynor, ed, *The Works of Oscar Wilde* (London, 1997), 656.
4 The queen's message to New York read in St Thomas's Church, 20 September 2001. See: 'Text of the Queen's message to New York', *The Guardian* (21 September 2001), accessed online 12 Apr. 2023. The original phrase is attributed to the British psychiatrist Colin Murray Parkes, in *Bereavement: Studies of Grief in Adult Life* (Madison, CT, 1972), 5.
5 Valentine Low, 'King Charles III: I pledge myself to you', *The Times* (10 September 2022).
6 'EL Doctorow' [obituary], *The Times* (23 July 2015).

Introduction: Taking the Pulse

1 Fernand Braudel, *A History of Civilizations* (London, 1995), xxxvi–xxxvii.
2 *Ibid.*
3 Peter Hennessy, *A Duty of Care: Britain Before and After Covid-19* (London, 2022).
4 House of Commons Committee of Public Accounts, *COVID 19: Cost Tracker Update*, HC 173 [report] (London, 25 July 2021), 3.
5 Social Mobility Commission, *State of the nation 2021: Social mobility and the pandemic* [report] (London, July 2021), xv.

6   Oliver Wright, 'Most people will still avoid parties, clubs and theatres despite end of Covid restrictions', *The Times* (19 July 2021).

7   Jeremy Farrar and Anjana Ahuja, *Spike – the Virus vs the People: The Inside Story* (London, 2021), 227.

8   The figures can be found at: https://coronavirus.data.gov.uk/details/cases. On 19 July, there were 47,924 recorded cases; 20 July: 39,877; 21 July: 35,548; 22 July: 31,278; 23 July: 27,817; 24 July: 22,852, 25 July: 22,187. On 26 July the number of cases rose to 29,980.

9   Peter Hennessy, interview with Michael Cockerell, BBC2, *Newsnight* (23 July 2019).

10 Peter Hennessy, interview with Michael Cockerell, BBC2, *Newsnight* (1 September 2022).

11 Peter Brookes, 'Short Supply', *The Times* (23 July 2021).

12 Andrew Blick and Peter Hennessy, *Good Chaps No More? Safeguarding the Constitution in Stressful Times* [report] (London, 2020).

13 Andrew Blick, *Electrified Democracy: The Internet and the United Kingdom Parliament in History* (Cambridge, 2021), 1.

14 Jenny McCartney, 'The dangers of Twitter', *UnHerd* (29 July 2021).

15 Fiona Harvey, 'Cool periods in UK are warmer than they used to be, say weather experts', *The Guardian* (28 July 2021).

16 Mike Kendon, et al., 'State of the UK Climate 2020', *International Journal of Climatology*, 41/S2 (July 2021), 3–4.

17 United Nations Intergovernmental Panel on Climate Change, *Climate Change 2021: The Physical Science Basis* [report] (9 August 2021).

18 He made these remarks during a Zoom meeting with some sixty northern Conservative MPs. See: 'Devolution "a disaster north of the border", says Boris Johnson', *The Guardian*, 16 November 2020 (accessed 16 Nov. 2021).

19 House of Lords Select Committee on the Constitution, 'Future governance of the UK' [oral evidence] (20 July 2021).

20 *Ibid.*

21 *Ibid.* (16 June 2021).

22 *Ibid.* (30 June 2021).

23 *Ibid.* (20 July 2021).

24 Gove is quoting Immanuel Kant's essay 'Idea for a Universal History with a Cosmopolitical Plan' [Ger. orig., *Idee zu einer allgemeinen Geschichte in weltbürgerlicher Absicht* (1784)].

25 House of Lords Select Committee on the Constitution, 'Future governance of the UK' [oral evidence] (20 July 2021).

26 House of Lords Select Committee on the Constitution, 'Revision of the *Cabinet Manual*' [oral evidence] (17 May 2021).

27 Peter Hennessy and Simon Coates, 'The Back of the Envelope: Hung Parliaments, the Queen and the Constitution', *Strathclyde Analysis Paper*, 5 (Strathclyde, 1991), 8.

28 Arthur Conan Doyle, 'The Adventure of the Sussex Vampire', *The Strand Magazine* (January 1924), 3.

29 BBC News at Six (5 August 2021).

30 John Ferguson, 'UK Government "will not stand in the way" of IndyRef2 forever says Michael Gove', *Sunday Mail* (1 August 2021).

31 Neil Pooran and Dave Miller, 'Alister Jack says Scottish independence referendum could happen if polling shows 60% support', *The Scotsman* (28 August 2021).

32 Gareth Southgate, 'Dear England', *The Player's Tribune* (8 June 2021).

33 Peter Hennessy, *Distilling the Frenzy: Writing the History of One's Own Times* (London, 2012), 23.

34 Hansard, HC vol 699, col 1282 (18 August 2021).

35 Amartya Sen, *Home in the World: A Memoir* (London, 2021), 32.

36 United Nations Intergovernmental Panel on Climate Change,

'Summary for Policymakers', *Climate Change 2021: The Physical Science Basis* (July 2021), 9.

37 *Ibid.*, 28.

38 *Ibid.*, 36.

39 Owen Mulhern, 'The Gulf Stream is Slowing: What are the Implications?', *Earth.org* (11 May 2021), accessed online 11 May 2021.

40 'Arctic Ice Melt is Changing Ocean Currents', *NASA* (6 February 2020).

41 IPCC, 'Summary for Policymakers', 36.

42 George Orwell, *Essays* (London, 2000), 78.

43 Gaylord Nelson, 'Earth Day 25 Years Later', *EPA Journal*, 21/1 (Winter 1995), 9.

1: An Autumn of Discontent

1 Lord O'Donnell, BBC Radio 4, *Today* (16 November 2021).

2 Sir Lindsay interviewed on BBC 2 *Newsnight* by Mark Urban (15 October 2021).

3 Keith Jeffrey and Peter Hennessy, *States of Emergency: British Governments and Strikebreaking since 1919* (London, 1983), 246.

4 Oliver Wright, 'Bailout is agreed to stop crisis reaching supermarket shelves', *The Times* (22 September 2021).

5 Robert Booth, Peter Walker, Steven Morris, 'Start full inquiry early, say Covid bereaved', *The Guardian* (13 October 2021).

6 Rob Davies, 'Blow to COP26 as China pushes coal and gas plan', *The Guardian* (13 October 2021).

7 David Brown, Ashley Armstrong, Oliver Wright, 'Backlog at biggest port forces ships to turn away', *The Times* (13 October 2021).

8 Henry Zeffman, 'We planned to break deal, says Cummings', *The Times* (14 October 2021).

9 House of Commons Health and Social Care Committee, and

Science and Technology Committee, *Coronavirus: lessons learned to date*, HC 92 [report] (London, 12 October 2021).

10 Public Health England, *The report on Exercise Alice: MERS-CoV* (15 February 2016), 2.

11 *Ibid.*, 9.

12 House of Commons Health and Social Care Committee, and Science and Technology Committee, 6.

13 *Ibid.*, 125.

14 *Ibid.*, 5.

15 'A great parliamentarian', *The Economist* (23 October 2021), 40.

16 Simon Case, 'Cabinet Secretary Lecture: Wednesday 13 October 2021', *Gov.uk* (14 October 2021), accessed online.

17 Henry Zeffman, 'Tory party facing identity crisis, says Portillo', *The Times* (29 October 2021).

18 Peter Hennessy, *Whitehall* (London, 1989), 120–8.

19 Simon Case.

20 *Ibid.*

21 See Hennessy, *Whitehall*, 120–68.

22 The Civil Service, *Vol. I: Report of the Committee 1966–68*, Cmnd 3638 (London, 1968).

23 Paul Johnson, 'Autumn budget 2021: Spending is splendid until it translates to reality', *The Times* (28 October 2021).

24 Zeffman.

25 House of Commons Committee on Standards, *Mr Owen Paterson: Third Report of Session 2021–22*, HC 797 (London, 26 October 2021), 5.

26 *Ibid.*, 48.

27 'Voting Intention: Con 35%, Lab 35% (3–4 Nov)', *YouGov* (4 November 2021), accessed online.

28 Lord Evans of Weardale made these remarks during a discussion with the director of the Institute for Government, Bronwen Maddox. See: Institute for Government, 'Keynote speech: Lord Evans, Chair of the Committee on Standards in

Public Life' [video], *YouTube* (4 November 2021), accessed online.

29 Private information.

30 Peter Hennessy, *The Hidden Wiring: Unearthing the British Constitution* (London, 1995), 181.

31 John Major, BBC Radio 4, *Today* (6 November 2021).

32 Michael Savage, 'Johnson's poll ratings slump to record low after lobbying affair', *The Observer* (7 November 2021).

33 Hansard, HC vol 703, cols 38–82 (8 November 2021).

34 'Footage appears to show Geoffrey Cox conducting legal work from Commons office' [video], *The Guardian* (10 November 2021).

35 John Stevens and Jason Grove, 'Now Boris pays the price at polls', *Daily Mail* (13 November 2021).

36 Chris Smyth, 'Two thirds of voters view Conservatives as very sleazy', *The Times* (13 November 2021).

37 Opinium/Observer poll, 'How would you describe the following people?', *The Observer* (14 November 2021).

38 Lord Butler of Brockwell, et al., 'Code of conduct' [letter], *The Times* (16 November 2021).

39 For the origins of the 'good chaps' theory of government see: Peter Hennessy and Andrew Blick, *Good Chaps No More? Safeguarding the Constitution in Stressful Times* [Constitution Society report] (London, 2020).

40 Boris Johnson, 'PM letter to the Speaker of the House of Commons on Parliamentary Standards', *Gov.uk* (16 November 2021), accessed online.

41 Hansard, HC vol 703, col 480 (16 November 2021).

42 Hansard, HC vol 703, col 572 (17 November 2021).

43 House of Commons Liaison Committee, *Oral Evidence from the Prime Minister*, HC 835 (17 November 2021).

44 Toby Helm and Michael Savage, 'Has Boris Johnson crashed the Tory car?', *The Observer* (21 November 2021).

45 Department of Transport, *Integrated Rail Plan for the North and the Midlands* (London, 18 November 2021).

46 Polly Rivers, 'A Year of the IRP: The highs (?), the lows and the really embarrassing U-turns', *Rail Insider* (18 November 2022).

47 Boris Johnson, interview with Krishnan Guru-Murthy, *Channel 4 News* (18 November 2021).

48 Vanessa Thorpe, 'Marr "wants to be free of BBC rules so he can speak out on climate"', *The Observer* (21 November 2021).

49 'The Times View: Pig's Ear', *The Times* (23 November 2021).

50 William Hague, 'There's still time for the Tories to get a grip', *The Times* (23 November 2021).

51 Private information.

52 Kate Bingham, 'Britain is driving away innovators in life sciences', *The Times* (23 November 2021).

53 *Ibid.*

54 Simon Case, 'Civil Service needs "more Dame Kates"', *The Times* (26 November 2021).

55 Chris Smyth, 'Public will not comply with any more restrictions, Whitty fears', *The Times* (27 November 2021).

56 'Prime Minister sets out new measures as Omicron variant identified in UK', *Gov.uk* (27 November 2021), accessed online.

57 Boris Johnson, BBC *News at Ten* (27 November 2021).

58 Dame Sarah Gilbert, 'Vaccine vs the Virus: This race and the next one', *The Richard Dimbleby Lecture*, BBC 1 (6 December 2021).

59 Toby Helm and Michael Savage, 'Johnson faces trust crisis as sleaze shatters faith in MPs', *The Observer* (5 December 2021).

60 Rowena Mason and Hannah Devlin, 'PM triggers Plan B as party scandal engulfs No.10', *The Guardian* (9 December 2021).

61 Tim Shipman. 'A Sticky Situation', *The Sunday Times* (2 January 2022).

62 Steven Swinford, Oliver Wright, Henry Zeffman, 'Poll

blow for Tories as trust in Boris Johnson falls', *The Times* (10 December 2021).

63 Toby Helm and Michael Savage, 'Labour races to nine-point lead in polls', *The Observer* (12 December 2021).

64 'Prime Minister's address to the nation on booster jabs', *Gov.uk* (12 December 2021), accessed online.

65 Queen Elizabeth II, BBC 1, *The Queen's Christmas Broadcast* (25 December 2021). For a transcript, see: 'The Christmas Broadcast 2021', *Royal.uk* (25 December 2021), accessed online.

66 Max Hastings, 'We shouldn't hanker for giants to lead us', *The Times* (24 December 2021).

67 Tom McTague, 'The Minister of Chaos', *The Atlantic* (July/ August 2021).

2: Who Belongs to Glasgow?

1 'Seer of the Anthropocene: Paul Crutzen died on January 28th', *The Economist* (13 February 2021), 62.

2 Jesse Norman, *Adam Smith: What He Thought and Why It Matters* (London, 2018), 15.

3 *Ibid.*

4 This description of Johnson emerged from the fluent pen of John Crace, political sketch-writer of *The Guardian*. See: John Crace, 'Boris "Bertie Booster" Johnson serves up climate baloney for breakfast', *The Guardian* (20 October 2021).

5 HM Government, *Net Zero Strategy: Build Back Greener* (London, 19 October 2021).

6 BBC *News at Ten* (21 September 2021).

7 Adam Vaughan, 'What to expect at COP26', *New Scientist* (30 October 2021).

8 World Meteorological Organization, *Greenhouse Gas Bulletin No.17* (25 October 2021).

9 Mark Carney, 'The world of finance will be judged by the $100bn climate challenge', *FT Weekend* (30–1 October 2021).

10 Arnold J. Toynbee, *A Study of History* (Oxford, 1948). For

Macmillan and Toynbee, see: Peter Hennessy, *Winds of Change: Britain in the Early Sixties* (London, 2019), 38–40.

11 Boris Johnson, interview with Beth Rigby, Sky News (30 October 2021).

12 Boris Johnson, interview with Laura Kuenssberg, BBC News at Six (30 October 2021).

13 'The Queen's Speech at the COP26 Evening Reception', *Royal. uk* (1 November 2021), accessed online.

14 Tom Ambrose, 'Attenborough urges leaders to "turn tragedy into triumph"', *The Guardian* (2 November 2021).

15 Oliver Milman, Nina Lakhani, 'Joe Biden, US is back at the table, president insists', *The Guardian* (2 November 2021).

16 Ben Webster, 'Loophole allows the coal fires to keep burning until 2050', *The Times* (3 November 2021).

17 Fiona Harvey, 'Global heating on track to top 2.4°C despite COP26 pledges, report warns', *The Guardian* (10 November 2021).

18 Oliver Wright and Ben Webster, 'US and China vow to limit warming together', *The Times* (10 November 2021).

19 Fiona Harvey, 'US and China announce surprise climate deal', *The Guardian* (10 November 2021).

20 Damian Carrington, 'Behavioural change key to ending crisis, Vallance says', *The Guardian* (10 November 2021).

21 Adam Vaughan, 'How the drama unfolded', *New Scientist* (20 November 2021).

22 Kaya Burgess and Steven Swinford, 'Cop26: We won. Now China and India will have to explain themselves', *The Times* (15 November 2021).

23 He was interviewed as part of BBC News' twenty-four-hour rolling coverage on the evening of Friday 12 November 2021.

3: Mr Johnson Helps the Police with Their Inquiries

1 Andrew Rawnsley, 'This is a Boris Johnson scandal that even

the great trickster can't blag his way out of', *The Guardian* (16 January 2022).

2   Private information.

3   Quoted in Henry Mance 'Johnson's government is "a bonfire of the decencies"', *Financial Times* (23 May 2022).

4   Boris Johnson, 'The Prime Minister's response to Lord Geidt, 21 December 2021', *Gov.uk* (6 January 2022), accessed online.

5   Lord Geidt, 'Letter from Lord Geidt to the Prime Minister, 17 December 2021', *Gov.uk* (6 January 2022), accessed online.

6   Lord Geidt, 'Lord Geidt's concluding letter to the Prime Minister, 23 December 2021', *Gov.uk* (6 January 2022), accessed online.

7   Steven Swinford, et al., 'Contrite? PM doesn't believe he did anything wrong, say Tories', *The Times* (13 January 2022).

8   Hansard, HC vol 706, col 562 (12 January 2022).

9   Hansard, HC vol 706, cols 564–5 (12 January 2022).

10 Charles Dickens, *A Tale of Two Cities* (Glasgow, 1912), 379.

11 Pippa Crerar, 'Boris' wine time Fridays', *Daily Mirror* (15 January 2022).

12 Toby Helm, 'Tories will oust PM if he tries to dodge "partygate" blame', *The Observer* (16 January 2022).

13 Rawnsley, *The Guardian*.

14 Hansard, HC vol 707, cols 322–4 (19 January 2022).

15 Hansard, HC vol 707, col 330 (19 January 2022); for Amery's speech, see: Hansard, HC vol 360, col 1150 (7 May 1940).

16 Boris Johnson, *The Churchill Factor: How One Man Made History* (London, 2014).

17 Hansard, HC vol 707, col 861 (25 January 2022).

18 Hansard, HC vol 704, col 909 (1 December 2021).

19 Hansard, HC vol 705, col 372 (8 December 2021).

20 Hansard, HC vol 707, col 995 (26 January 2022).

21 *Ibid.*, col 997.

22 Matthew Weaver, '"Nobody is above the law": Theresa May

Wades into Downing Street parties row', *The Guardian* (28 January 2022).

23 'Wrecking ball', *The Economist* (29 January 2022).

24 Andrew Neil, Channel 4, *The Andrew Neil Show* (30 January 2022).

25 Cabinet Office [investigation conducted by Sue Gray], *Investigation into Alleged Gatherings on Government Premises During COVID Restrictions – Update* (London, 31 January 2022).

26 Tanya Gold, 'The Man Trying to Take Down Boris Johnson', *New York Magazine* (30 January 2022).

27 Jessica Elgot, 'Cummings: "It's my duty to get rid of the PM, it's like fixing the drains"', *The Guardian* (31 January 2022).

28 Cabinet Office.

29 Hansard, HC vol 708, col 23 (31 January 2022).

30 *Ibid.*, cols 24–5.

31 *Ibid.*, col 26.

32 *Ibid.*, col 26.

33 Hansard, HC vol 708, col 147 (1 February 2022).

34 Oliver Ward, Henry Zeffman, Steven Swinford, '"Scurrilous" smear is last straw for long-time ally of Johnson', *The Times* (4 February 2022).

35 BBC2, *Newsnight* (3 February 2022).

36 BBC *Six O'Clock News* (3 February 2022).

37 'Gray day, Gray day', *The Economist* (5 February 2022).

38 Martin Kettle, 'Like Trump, Johnson is dismantling democracy', *The Guardian* (4 February 2022).

39 Steven Swinford, Oliver Wright, Henry Zeffman, 'Civil war in Cabinet as PM told to sack Sunak', *The Times* (5 February 2022).

40 Tim Shipman and Caroline Wheeler, 'Vengeful cabinet turns on "plotter" Sunak as succession rumours intensify', *The Sunday Times* (6 February 2022).

41 Sir Max Hastings, 'Has this experiment in celebrity

government given us the most disreputable leader in history?',
The Sunday Times (6 February 2022).

42 Labour MP Chris Bryant speaking on *Channel 4 News* [video]
(7 February 2022).

43 Hansard, HC vol 708, col 783 (8 February 2022).

44 John Major, 'In democracy we trust? A keynote speech by The
Rt Hon Sir John Major', *Institute for Government* (10 February
2022), accessed online.

45 *Ibid.*

46 A. J. P. Taylor, *The Struggle for Mastery in Europe 1849–1918*
(Oxford, 1954).

47 Tim Shipman, 'Half the cabinet's seats now at risk, reveals new
poll', *The Sunday Times* (27 February 2022).

48 See, for example: Fiona Harvey, 'IPCC issues "bleakest
warning yet" on impacts of climate breakdown', *The Guardian*
(1 March 2022).

49 Neal Ascherson, 'History replays like a half-forgotten song,
but once we remember, it's far too late', *The Observer* (6 March
2022).

50 Conversation with author, early March 2022.

51 'Remarks by President Biden at the House Democratic Caucus
Issues Conference', *The White House* (11 March 2022), accessed
online.

52 Daniel Boffey, 'EU leaders announce intention to collectively
rearm in face of Putin threat', *The Guardian* (12 March 2022).

53 Toby Helm and Daniel Boffey, 'Fury greets Boris Johnson's
claim Ukraine fight is like Brexit', *The Observer* (20 March
2022).

54 *Ibid.*

55 Lord Cormack, 'Comparing Ukraine's fight to the Brexit vote'
[letter], *The Times* (22 March 2022).

56 Hansard, HC vol 711, col 807 (30 March 2022).

57 Pippa Crerar, 'Partygate scandal: Now PM is facing more fines',
Daily Mirror (18 April 2022).

58 Daniel Finkelstein, 'How we can fix our constitutional crisis', *The Times* (20 April 2022).

59 Marina Hyde, 'There is no pooper scooper big enough for Boris Johnson's mess', *The Guardian* (20 April 2022).

60 Hansard, HC vol 712, col 63 (19 April 2022).

61 Heather Stewart, Aubrey Allegretti, 'MPs should wait for "full facts" on Partygate, says Johnson in India', *The Guardian* (21 April 2022).

4: The Twenty-Four Steps

1 Private information.

2 R. H. Tawney, 'The Choice before the Labour Party', *The Political Quarterly*, 3/3 (July/September 1932), 323.

3 Max Hastings, 'Who should be prime minister? Anyone but Boris Johnson', *The Guardian* (14 May 2022).

4 Keir Starmer on police ending Downing Street parties inquiry [video], BBC News (19 May 2022).

5 Cabinet Office, *Findings of Second Permanent Secretary's Investigation into Alleged Gatherings on Government Premises During COVID* Restrictions [report] (London, 25 May 2022).

6 Hansard, HC vol 715, col 299 (25 May 2022).

7 Cabinet Office, 13–16.

8 'The Times view on Sue Gray's findings: Party Politics', *The Times* (25 May 2022).

9 Hansard, HC vol 715, col 298 (25 May 2022).

10 Robert Peston on the Gray Report, ITV *News at 10* (25 May 2022).

11 Oliver Wright, et al., 'Sue Gray report vindicates me over No. 10 parties, claims Boris Johnson', *The Times* (27 May 2022).

12 Andrew Rawnsley, 'Boris Johnson, the party animal, has vomited over standards in public life', *The Observer* (29 May 2022).

13 Jeremy Wright, 'The Prime Minister May 2022' [blog post],

Jeremy Wright MP for Kenilworth and Southam (30 May 2022), accessed online.

14 'A Tory leadership ballot could come as soon as next week, William Hague' [video interview], *Times Radio* (broadcast 31 May 2022).

15 Lord Geidt, 'Preface' in *Independent Adviser on Ministers' Interests: Annual Report 2021–2022* (London, May 2022), 4.

16 Boris Johnson, 'Letter from the Prime Minister to the Independent Adviser on Ministers' Interests', *Gov.uk* (31 May 2022), accessed online.

17 Former attorney general Dominic Grieve speaks with Ayshah Tull on *Channel 4 News* [video interview] (31 May 2022).

18 Steven Swinford, Patrick Maguire, Henry Zeffman, 'Lord Geidt threatens to resign as Boris Johnson's ethics chief', *The Times* (1 June 2022).

19 'Mumsnet founder Justine Roberts puts users' questions to Prime Minister Boris Johnson', *Mumsnet* (4 July 2022), accessed online.

20 Daniel Finkelstein, 'PM can't ignore the booing – they should be his crowd', *The Times* (4 June 2022).

21 Charlotte Wace, Lucy Bannerman, 'Queen's thanksgiving service: Boos and jeers for Boris Johnson outside St Paul's', *The Times* (4 June 2022).

22 Queen Elizabeth II, 'A thank you message from Her Majesty The Queen following the Platinum Jubilee weekend', *Royal.uk* (5 June 2022), accessed online.

23 Tim Shipman, 'Can Johnson weather the coming storm?' *The Sunday Times* (5 June 2022).

24 Jesse Norman, 'Governments must step up to the mark and clean our rivers' [blog post], *Jesse Norman* (9 June 2022), accessed online.

25 BBC *News at Ten* (6 June 2022).

26 William Hague, 'Johnson should look for an honourable exit', *The Times* (7 June 2022).

27 BBC *News at Ten* (7 June 2022).

28 Hansard, HC vol 715, col 800 (8 June 2022); Johnson was seen to mutter 'not even a flesh wound' in response to a comment by the SNP's Ian Blackford, comparing him to the delusional and ultimately defenceless Black Knight from the film *Monty Python and the Holy Grail* – see Lizzy Buchan, 'Boris Johnson boasts "not even a flesh wound" as he's compared to Monty Python's Black Knight', *The Mirror* (8 June 2022), accessed online 8 June 2022.

29 'Times Letters: Day of reckoning beckons for Boris Johnson', *The Times*, 8 June 2022.

30 Jesse Norman, 'Britain under Boris Johnson has abandoned ideals of political leadership', *Financial Times* (10 June 2022).

31 Jesse Norman, *Edmund Burke: Philosopher, Politician, Prophet* (London, 2013).

32 Norman, 'Britain under Boris Johnson'.

33 Public Administration and Constitutional Affairs Committee, 'Oral Evidence: The Independent Adviser on Ministerial Interests', HC 40 (14 June 2022).

34 'Correspondence from Lord Geidt and the Prime Minister's response', *Gov.uk* (15 June 2022), accessed online.

35 Andrew Marr, 'What the US Capitol riot hearings teach us about the slow decay of political norms', *New Statesman* (15 June 2022).

36 Clare Foges, 'Johnson is neither good chap nor great man', *The Times* (22 June 2022).

37 Dowden tweeted a copy of his resignation letter early on Friday morning, 24 June 2022.

38 Michael Howard talking to Jonny Dymond, BBC Radio 4, *World at One* (24 June 2022).

39 William Hague, 'Johnson should look for an honourable exit', *The Times* (7 June 2022).

40 BBC Radio 4, *Today* (7 June 2022).

41 Speaking to reporters on the final day of the Commonwealth Heads of Government Meeting in Kigali, Rwanda.

42 'Rishi Sunak's resignation letter and the Prime Minister's response', *Gov.uk* (5 July 2022), accessed online.

43 'Sajid Javid's resignation letter and the Prime Minister's response', *Gov.uk* (5 July 2022), accessed online.

44 Matthew Smith, 'Snap poll: most Conservative voters now want Boris Johnson to resign', *YouGov* (5 July 2022).

45 Sebastian Payne, *The Fall of Boris Johnson: The Full Story* (London, 2022), 207.

46 *Ibid.*, 207–8.

47 *Ibid.*, 208.

48 *Ibid.*, 208.

49 *Ibid.*, 209.

50 *Ibid.*, 220–21.

51 Sidney Low, *The Governance of England* (London, 1904), 12.

52 W. E. Gladstone, *The Gleanings of Past Years*, vol. 1 (London, 1879), 245.

5: Hustings Inside a Heat Dome

1 Ferdinand Mount, *Big Caesars and Little Caesars: How They Rise and How They Fall – From Julius Caesar to Boris Johnson* (London, 2023), 234.

2 Hansard, HC vol 718, col 322 (13 July 2022).

3 Public Administration and Constitutional Affairs Committee, 'Propriety of governance in light of Greensill' [inquiry], HC 212 (12 July 2022).

4 *Ibid.*

5 *Ibid.*

6 Hansard, HC vol 718, col 726–33 (18 July 2022).

7 Daniel Finkelstein, 'Time to cut members out of Tory leadership', *The Times* (20 July 2022).

8 Andrew Marr, 'As the Tory leadership candidates obsess over

tax cuts, the real monsters are tapping at the window', *New Statesman* (15–21 July 2022).

9 Caroline Wheeler and Harry Yorke, 'Is our most maverick PM really aiming for a sequel?' *The Sunday Times* (24 July 2022).

10 Andrew Rawnsley, 'Liz Truss reminds me of a Tory leader but it's not Margaret Thatcher', *The Observer* (24 July 2022).

11 William Hague, 'Tories must beware Boris the incredible sulk', *The Times* (26 July 2022).

12 Frances Gibb, 'Lord Mackay: Margaret Thatcher stuck to the rules. Boris Johnson didn't', *The Times* (30 July 2022).

13 Matt Dathan, 'My removal is greatest stitch-up since Bayeux Tapestry, Boris Johnson tells wedding party guests', *The Times* (1 August 2022).

14 Isobel Frodsham, 'Mark Drakeford is a "low energy Jeremy Corbyn", Tory leadership contender says', *The Independent* (4 August 2022).

15 Blair Worden, 'Man with a mission', *The Spectator* (14 July 2007), 27.

16 Toby Helm, 'Poll of Tory members gives Liz Truss 22-point lead to be next prime minister', *The Observer* (14 August 2022).

17 Will Hutton, 'Liz Truss's economic plan is ruinous nonsense with no reference to reality', *The Observer* (14 August 2022).

18 Severin Carrell, 'Sunak and Truss rule out freezing energy prices at leadership hustings', *The Guardian* (17 August 2022). Liz Truss tweeted: 'I will make sure that now and forever, our fantastic Union goes from strength, to strength, to strength' (16 August 2022).

19 Pippa Crerar, 'Leaked audio reveals Liz Truss said British workers needed "more graft"', *The Guardian* (17 August 2022).

20 Steven Swinford, Henry Zeffman, 'Truss plans are holiday from reality, says Gove', *The Times* (20 August 2022).

21 Matthew Parris, 'There's no more to Truss than meets the eye', *The Times* (20 August 2022).

22 Burt made this remark on Twitter: 'This is a desperately serious

error, which the FS should take back. The better answer would have been "of course he and France are friends and allies, both in NATO and the cause of freedom: it doesn't mean we don't have our differences and need to talk honestly, as I will'" (25 August 2022).

23 Barwell posted this remark on Twitter (25 August 2022).

24 Gauke posted this remark on Twitter (25 August 2022).

25 Andrew Rawnsley, 'Sunak and Truss care more about their small differences than the crises facing Britain', *The Observer* (28 August 2022).

26 George Grylls, 'Liz Truss's plan to cut VAT would crash economy, warns expert', *The Times* (29 August 2022).

6: Operation London Bridge

1 Quoted unattributably in Ben Pimlott, *The Queen: Elizabeth II and the Monarchy* (Golden Jubilee edn., London, 2002), 700–1.

2 James Forsyth, 'Energy bill crisis could finish this Tory era', *The Times* (2 September 2022).

3 J. K. Galbraith, *The Affluent Society* (fortieth anniversary edn, London, 1998) 9.

4 'Statement from The King following the death of the queen', *Royal.uk* (8 September 2022), accessed online.

5 'His Majesty The King's address to the Nation and Commonwealth' *Royal.uk* (9 September 2022), accessed online.

6 'His Majesty The King's Declaration', *Royal.uk* (10 September 2022), accessed online.

7 'His Majesty The King's reply to addresses of condolence at Westminster Hall', *Royal.uk* (published 12 September 2022), accessed online.

Epilogue: Was there an Elizabethan Era?

1 Lytton Strachey, *Queen Victoria* (London, 2006), 265.

2 Keir Starmer, 'Broadcast statement from the Leader of the Opposition', *Labour* (8 September 2022), accessed online.

3 Craig Taylor, 'Uppies win first game of the season', *The Orcadian* (27 December 2018).

4 Private information.

5 Private information.

6 Hannah Furness, 'Queen: UK must overcome "deeply held differences"', *The Daily Telegraph* (24 December 2018).

7 Conversation with Professor Philip Ogden (19 December 2018).

8 'TV ratings for Queen's Christmas Speech drop by one million, amid suggestions Netflix could be to blame', *The Telegraph* (27 December 2018).

9 Quoted in Robert Hardman, *Queen of the World*, (London, 2018), 260.

10 Antony Jay, ed, *The Oxford Dictionary of Political Quotations*, (Oxford, 2006), 185.

11 Andrew Blick and Peter Hennessy, *The Bonfire of the Decencies: Repairing and Restoring the British Constitution* (London, 2022).

Postscript: There May Be Trouble Ahead

1 Lord Rothschild, *Meditations on a Broomstick* (London, 1977), 163.

2 Irving Berlin, 'Let's Face the Music and Dance' in *Follow the Fleet* [film] (1936).

3 Steven Swinford, 'Truss decides against sacking Case', *The Times* (12 September 2022).

Picture Sources

Page 189   Queen Elizabeth II and the Duke of Edinburgh in
            a Morris van after a visit to Pierowall Junior High
            School on Westray, Orkney Islands, 12 August 1960.
            Source: The Orcadian, OA Ref: L1138/1.
Page 199   Chancellor of the Exchequer Kwasi Kwarteng
            leaves 11 Downing Street after accepting the prime
            minister's request that he 'stand aside,' paying the
            price for the chaos unleashed by his mini-budget, 14
            October 2022. Source: Alamy.

Index

The Times 3, 4, 33, 35, 36–7,
47, 66, 85, 103, 112, 116, 118,
122–3, 160–61, 164, 167–8
Times Radio 28, 114, 122
Timmermans, Frans 55, 58
Truss, Liz
  Cabinet appointments 172
  and Charles III 178
  and death of Queen
    Elizabeth 175, 183
  economic policy 199–203
  elected Prime Minister
    168–70, 171
  in-tray 170
  leadership campaign 144–7,
    148, 149, 150, 152, 153,
    154–5, 157, 158, 159–60
  Truss premiership misgivings
    156–7, 158–9, 160–62,
    164–5, 202–3
Tugendhat, Tom 11–12, 143–4,
  145, 146
Turnbull, Lord (Andrew) 33
Tusk, Donald 99

U
Ukraine *see* Russo-Ukrainian
  war (2022)
United Nations, IPCC reports
  6, 14, 16, 94
United States
  climate change 51, 57, 58–9
  coal-fired power stations 55,
    56

and Ukraine 90, 96

V
Vallance, Sir Patrick 37, 38, 41,
  57–8
Varadkar, Leo 21
Verhofstadt, Guy 99

W
Wakeford, Christian 71
Waldegrave, Lord (William)
  182
Welby, Justin, Archbishop 173,
  180, 183–4, 187
Wheatcroft, Patience 170
Wheeler, Caroline 86
Whitty, Sir Chris 37–8, 41, 45
Wilson, Lord (Richard) 33
Wishart, Peter 101
Wragg, William 134, 142–3
Wright, Ben 108
Wright, Jeremy 114
Wright, Lord (Patrick) 97

X
Xi Jinping 51

Y
Young, Sir Edward 136, 177
Young, Vicki 102, 103

Z
Zahawi, Nadhim 136, 143–4
Zelensky, Volodymyr 139